Rothman Foundation Series

JEP

לשמור ולעשות

A GUIDE TO BASIC PRINCIPLES OF JEWISH LAW AND THEIR APPLICATIONS IN THEORY AND IN PRACTICE

Rabbi Mordechai Katz

© Copyright 1981 by
JEP PUBLICATIONS

JEWISH EDUCATION PROGRAM
425 East 9th Street
Brooklyn, New York 11218
212-941-2600

First printing September 1981

Sole Trade Distributors
PHILIPP FELDHEIM, INC.
96 East Broadway
New York, N.Y. 10002

FELDHEIM PUBLISHERS Ltd.
POB 6525
Jerusalem, Israel

ISBN # 0-87306-974-9

In memory of

Maurice M. Rothman ז״ל

לחם מלחמות ה׳

*"who lived and fought
for Torah-true Judaism"*

Published through the courtesy of the
HENRY, BERTHA and EDWARD ROTHMAN FOUNDATION
Rochester, N.Y. • Circleville, Ohio • Cleveland

Jewish Education Program

The Joseph & Faye Tanenbaum Jewish Education Program of Zeirei Agudath Israel was organized in September 1972, and since its inception has become a well-known, active force in the field of Jewish education. Its guiding principle, "Jewish power and Jewish pride through Jewish education," was formulated in response to what has become a Jewish tragedy of massive proportions, namely assimilation and its tragic by-products.

Under the guidelines of prominent Roshei Yeshivos and leaders in the field of Jewish education, and staffed entirely by B'nei Torah and Yeshiva graduates, JEP relies almost entirely on the talents and efforts voluntarily contributed by capable young Torah students.

Some of JEP's programs include: Shabbatones, in which hundreds of children from various communities in the United States and Canada experience the beauty of Shabbos in a Torah true environment; Release Hour classes for spiritually-starved public school children; programs for needy Russian immigrants; Ruach and Seminar sessions for day school students; Chavruso Big Brother Programs; High School Encounter Groups; Holiday Rallies; Yeshiva and Camp Placement; and the publication of educational material for thousands of young people. Through these and other various programs, JEP hopes to ignite the spark of Yiddishkeit deep within the hearts of these individuals, and turn it into a blazing, warmth-emanating fire. It hopes to instill within these youngsters a love of Hashem and His Torah and an understanding of Torah-true Judaism.

All proceeds of this Sefer will go to benefit JEP's various Kiruv projects which have been instrumental in the placement of over 1,000 children into Yeshivos, Hebrew Day Schools, and Camps.

ACKNOWLEDGEMENTS

At this juncture, I would like to express my deepest feelings of gratitude to those who have graciously given of themselves and their time to help me in this holy endeavor.

I would first of all wish to express thanks to, my parents, Mr. and Mrs. Moshe Katz, and my in-laws, Mr. and Mrs. Yitzchok Berger, and all the members of my family for their encouragement and support. May *Hashem* grant them long life and *nachas* from their offspring.

An undertaking such as this must be guided by *Gedolei Torah*. I would, therefore, like to thank: Horav Yisroel Belsky, *Shlita*, Rosh Yeshiva, Yeshiva Torah Vodaath; Horav Reuven Feinstein, *Shlita*, Rosh Yeshiva, Mesifta Tiferes Yerusholayim; Horav Shlomo Frankel, *Shlita*, Horav Elazar Kahana, *Shlita*, Rosh Yeshiva, Yeshiva Torah Vodaath; and Horav Leibel Katz, *Shlita*, Rav of Khal Zichron Yosef. I would like to thank these people for reading the material, reviewing the *Halachos*, and offering comments and suggestions which have been incorporated into the text. I am humbly grateful for their efforts.

I would like to thank the following *chaverim* who assisted in the writing and editing of the work, and without whose tireless efforts this volume never would have become reality: Rabbi Eliezer Gevirtz, talented writer of the *Sefer, Lehovin Ulehaskil*; Bezalel Lerner and Dovid Zwiebel.

Special thanks and deepest appreciation to Rabbi Yosef Chaim Golding, who put in countless hours and exceptional effort in reviewing this work and seeing to it that it was properly produced and made available to the public.

I would like to thank Mrs. Malky Bodenstein and Mrs. Chavy Aranoff who assisted in the writing and typing of the manuscript.

I would like to thank Malya Karmel for proofreading, typing and technical advice.

We are greatly indebted to the members of the Henry, Bertha, and Edward Rothman Foundation for sponsoring this publication. May *Hashem* grant them continued success in all of their worthy endeavors and may they continue to spread Jewish education to those who so desperately need it.

Special thanks to . . .

Nutty Goldbrenner and Shiya Markowitz of the Goldmark Group, for their invaluable technical assistance.

Mr. Max Septimus for allowing us to utilize his priceless library collection for the front covers of JEP's educational series.

Mr. Samuel Shpelfogel for his technical assistance.

Mrs. Judy Dick, Feigy Gurkov, Moshe Friedman, Yaakov Rosen, Dr. Phil Abramowitz and Yitzchok Feldheim for their proofreading and suggestions.

I would like to express my deepest gratitude to, and reverence for, my *Rebbeim* and *Roshei HaYeshiva*, for their guidance and encouragement throughout the years.

These people's interest and inspiration are what made this publication possible. May they continue to devote their supreme abilities to the furtherance of *Yiddishkeit* and may *Hashem* grant them the spiritual well-being that they so richly deserve.

My deepest gratitude and appreciation goes to my wife, Pessi, for her support, self-sacrifice, and dedication. Without her this work never would have been completed. May her sincere and untiring efforts be rewarded in the blessing most precious to her—that our children merit to sit in the House of *Hashem*.

I humbly thank the *Ribono Shel Olam* for permitting me to accomplish this task.

Rabbi M. Katz
Sivan, 5741

PREFACE

רבי ישמעל בנו אומר הלומד על מנת ללמד, מספיקין בידו
ללמוד וללמד; והלומד על מנת לעשות, מספיקין בידו ללמוד
וללמד, לשמור ולעשות.

*Rabbi Yishmael his son (Rabbi Yochanon ben Broko's son)
said, He who learns in order to teach will be granted [by
Hashem] the means both to learn and to teach; but he who
learns in order to practice, [Hashem] will grant him the opportunity to learn and to teach, to observe and to perform.* (Avos
4:5)

The Chasam Sofer offers the following interpretation of Rabbi Yishmael's dictum: He who sets time aside in order to teach others is granted
the extraordinary power to excel in both learning and teaching. He who
learns with the even loftier ideal of putting his learning to practical use
merits the blessings of *Hashem*, which will enable him to achieve promi-
nence in each of the exalted forms of Jewish service—learning, teaching,
and doing.

It is significant that the words *Lishmor Vela'asos* ("to observe and to
do [the laws]") appear after those of *Lehovin Ulehaskil* ("to understand
and to comprehend") and *Lilmod Ulelamed* ("to learn and to teach") in
the morning prayers. A Jew is called upon to gain a sound foundation in
Jewish theory, and learning, to spread those teachings among his
brethren, and ultimately, as the highest expression of G-dly service, to
synthesize abstract theory and practical action by performing the *Mitzvos* with a full understanding of their meaning and details.

Throughout the years, many Jews have challenged the need for
religious laws. They have claimed that they could survive as Jews just as
easily without the "burden" of the *Mitzvos*. They are wrong. Without the
practical application of ideals via the *Mitzvos*, Judaism would operate
merely in the abstract. It would have no concrete foundation at all.
Those Jews who have abandoned Jewish law have all too frequently
abandoned Judaism as well. Therefore, it is natural that *Shemira* and
Asiyah should be an essential complement to *Havonoh* and *Limud*.

And it is likewise only natural that this third volume in the JEP series of
Torah publications be devoted to the practical application of Jewish law.

The Torah concepts described in *Lilmod Ulelamed* and the Jewish philosophy discussed in *Lehovin Ulehaskil* reach their culmination in the *Mitzvos* and *Dinim* detailed in *Lishmor Vela'asos*. Those who perform G-d's laws eagerly and meticulously show that they have gained insight into G-d's plan for man.

This volume is a summary of the most commonly applied *halochos* in the *Shulchan Oruch, Orach Chaim,* as elaborated in the *Mishnah Brurah,* and parts of *Yorah De'ah.* It includes recent halachic decisions from some of the foremost Rabbinical authorities of our day.

Like *Lilmod Ulelamed,* this volume offers a series of stories and *ma'amorei Chazal* that provide an additional dimension to the discussion of the laws. These are intended as background material to the *dinim,* bringing to life the spirit of the law, and showing its practical effect on man's faith and morals.

It should be stressed that Jewish law is very complex, and that this small volume is merely an overview and introduction into the vast world of *halacha.* The reader is strongly urged to refer to the original texts of the major *Sifrei Halacha* and to consult his local Rabbinical authority in cases of doubt. Nonetheless, we are confident that this book will serve the needs of a varied group of readers; the layman who cannot easily consult the primary halachic sources; the student wishing to understand the practical applications of the law; and the teacher seeking ways to present halachic teachings in a dramatic fashion.

It is our prayer that *Lishmor Vela'asos* will increase Jewish allegiance to Torah law and appreciation of its wisdom, so that the Jewish people will remain faithful to the ways of the *Avos* (Fathers) and ensure the speedy coming of the *Moshiach.*

TABLE OF CONTENTS

השכמת הבקר
Hashkomas Haboker

INTRODUCTION—HASHKOMAS HABOKER

A person who awakens in the morning is similar to a new creature who requires purification, as it is written: "They (the souls) are new every morning" (Lam. 3:23) It is, therefore, incumbent upon every man to purify himself and wash his hands out of a vessel upon awakening. (Beth Yosef, Ch. 4).

HILCHOS HASHKOMAS HABOKER
The Laws of Rising In The Morning

I. RULES OF MORNING CONDUCT

1. Upon rising in the morning, one should resolve to conduct himself during the day in accordance with the principle of, "I always place *Hashem* (G-d) before me." *(Psalms)* This means that one should always sense that he is in the presence of *Hashem,* Who is aware of all his actions and he must therefore behave accordingly.

TEFILLAH

It is important for us to realize that it is not for *Hashem*'s sake that we pray. Rather, the purpose of *Tefillah* is to give us a chance for introspection and self-analysis, and to make us realize that *Hashem* is the only one who can and does provide us with all our needs. We must always remember to be humble before *Hashem* and to thank Him for what He grants us.

Tefillah involves much more than simply worshipping *Hashem* or requesting our daily needs. It is one of the important means that we as human beings have of establishing a personal relationship with the Almighty. Prayer makes it possible for man to pour out his heart before G-d without any intermediaries. No matter how unimportant one thinks he is, he is always welcome to communicate directly with the Almighty.

There is no better means of approaching the L-rd than through prayer, for in the very hour that Jews pray and praise the L-rd, lifting their eyes and hearts toward Heaven, the Holy One, blessed be He, looks down upon them with Divine mercy and is overjoyed to hear their voices. The L-rd awaits, as it were, His children's prayers, and as soon as they address Him, He is most eager to respond to them. Said R. Zera: "A man may have a loving friend, but as soon as he asks him a

2. One should try to rise quickly, indicating that he is eager to perform the desired commandments of *Hashem*.

II. MODEH ANI

1. *Modeh Ani* is recited upon awakening in the morning. One should pause between the words *"B'Chemlo"* and *"Rabba"* to avoid mixing the phrases *"Shehe'chezarta Bee Nishmosee B'chemlo"* and *"Rabba Emunosecha."* *Modeh Ani* is a declaration of recognition of *Hashem's* kindness to us in restoring our souls to our bodies and renewing our vigor. The last two words, *"Rabbo Emunosecho,"* constitute a separate sentence meaning, "Great is Your faithfulness."

2. *Raishis Chochma,* the second part of *Modeh Ani,* contains *Hashem's* name and should not be recited until after one has washed *Netilas Yodayim.* The reason for this is that a person's hands are considered impure after he has arisen from sleep and they must, therefore, be purified by washing before one pronounces *Hashem's* name. Since the first paragraph of *Modeh Ani* does not contain *Hashem's* name, it may be said immediately upon awakening, even before washing one's hands.

III. NETILAS YODAYIM UPON AWAKENING

1. Men, women and children are required to perform the *Mitzvah* of *Netilas Yodayim* (washing one's hands) upon awakening in the morning.

favor or needs his help, he turns to be his enemy and rebuffs him. But, the Holy One, blessed be He, appreciates a man more when he begs, invokes and prays. The L-rd even invites man, as it were, to pray to Him."

Prayer is also refuge from disappointment and despair. As both R. Yochanan and R. Eleazar said, "Even if a sharp sword rests on a man's neck, he should not desist from prayer." *(Brochos)*

Another vital purpose of *Tefillah* is to teach us not to be selfish—not to pray only for ourselves. Our prayers link our thoughts and desires with the yearnings of Jews all over the world, and with the needs of all mankind as well.

This is also seen as one of the reasons that we pray in Hebrew, rather than in the language of the country in which we reside. We want our *Tefillos* to be international, for the good of *Klal Yisroel* wherever they are. Therefore, we use the historic Hebrew language that unites all Jews in all countries throughout the generations.

Most of the *Tefillos* are phrased in the collective "we" and refer to each person's membership in *Klal Yisroel.* Once we learn to pray for the greater good of all, we become more deserving of a positive response to our own personal pleas. We also learn to request intelligent and meaningful things.

Man stands bewildered amidst a mighty Universe, and like a frightened child he calls to his Father in prayer. Man struggles with fear and afflic-

13

It is proper to do so before walking *Daled Amos* (4 cubits or approximately 7 feet).

2. One should wash with a *Reviyis* (3.3 or 4.4 ounces of water, depending on different authorities.) The water should reach till the wrist. If this is not possible (like on *Yom Kippur*) the water must still reach till the knuckles. The laws that apply to the kind of vessel used for washing before a meal should also be followed for the morning *Netilas Yodayim*. For example, a cup that cannot stand by itself or one that is cracked should not be used for washing in the morning. If one does not have a *Reviyis* of water, or there is no other vessel available except for the kind stated above, he should wash with what he has.

3. The water should not be spilled on the floor, but rather, into a basin. Thereafter it should not be used for any purpose, including washing another person's hands.

4. If one has not prepared water and an accompanying basin within reach of one's bed, and there is no one to bring them to him, he may go to the nearest source of water in order to wash his hands, even if it's beyond the prescribed limit of *Daled Amos* (about 7 feet). The best thing to do is to proceed to the source of water as quickly and directly as possible without stopping along the way. Some consider this as having fulfilled the requirement of *Daled Amos*. One opinion holds one's entire house to be within the limit of *Daled Amos* since the entire area is covered by one

tions and cries for help in prayer.

Man longs for peace and happiness and begs for them in prayer.

A man who has achieved his aim or was delivered from danger intones his thanks in prayer.

A man recognizes his lowliness and worthlessness and seeks support and encouragement in prayer.

A man calls to mind the Day of Judgment and asks forgiveness in prayer.

Tefillah is the Hebrew word for judgment. Prayer is the worshipper's appeal to G-d to judge him with mercy and compassion. (Abudraham)

THE SIDDUR

The one *sefer* (Hebrew book) that is perhaps most familiar to every Jew is the *Siddur,* our book of *Tefillos* from which we *daven* (pray) every day. The *Siddur* is a priceless treasure that has served the Jewish people for more than a thousand years. It is universal among Jews. Wherever one travels throughout the world, in any synagogue he may enter, he will find that the *Siddur* is essentially the same. The *Tefillos* have not been substantially changed since the *Siddur* was first compiled in the year 858 C.E., during the Gaonic period.

The various *Tefillos* were composed by the *Anshei Knesses Hagdolah* (members of the Great Assembly) and others, since the time of the second *Bais Hamikdosh.* However, it had

roof, but one should depend on this opinion only when necessary.

5. If no water is available at all, one should rub his hands on sand, wood, or other material, and recite the *Brocho, "Al Nekiyus Yodayim"* (instead of *"Al Netilas Yodayim"*).

6. One may not touch his mouth, nose, ears and eyes or any open wound before washing *Netilas Yodayim*. Similarly, he may not touch food. However, if he did, the food is not considered forbidden to be eaten. A Jew may eat food touched by a non-Jew who does not wash his hands.

7. One should not have his hands washed by someone else who has not yet washed his own hands. For example, a mother who helps her children wash in the morning, should be sure to wash her own hands first.

8. If one naps during the day for more than half an hour, he should wash his hands three times, alternating them, without reciting any *Brocho*.

IV. ONE SHOULD ALSO WASH HIS HANDS IN THE FOLLOWING INSTANCES:

1. After leaving the toilet,
2. After cutting one's hair or nails,
3. After touching one's shoes, or a part of the body that is usually covered,

been forbidden to write down any part of the various *Tefillos*, as they were considered part of the *Torah She-Ba'al Peh* (the Oral Law that was not permitted to be transcribed).

The person who finally saw the need for compiling and arranging the *Siddur* was Rav Amrom Gaon, who headed the *Yeshiva* in Sura, Babylonia and who received the title of "Gaon" in 858 C.E. Rav Amrom was most famous for his *Teshuvos* (Responsae)—answers to questions of Jewish law. He sent these replies to members of the growing Jewish communities throughout Spain, who were constantly turning to the Babylonian *Yeshivos* to help clarify problems of Jewish law.

It was in response to a request by the Jews of Barcelona, Spain, that he compiled his famous *Siddur*, the first organized book of prayers the Jews ever had. Because of the exile and persecutions of the Jews, he was afraid that the prayers would be forgotten so he wrote them down. From Barcelona, the *Siddur* is believed to have passed on to the communities in Arab Spain, and from there to the rest of Europe, where it was widely studied and quoted by the Rambam, Rabbeinu Tam, and others.

The word *"Siddur"* is similar to the word *"Seder,"* which means "order." The *Siddur* has all the prayers arranged in a special order. If one looks at the Table of Contents in a *Siddur*, one finds a long list of prayers for

4. After scratching one's head,

5. After touching insects,

6. After being in contact with a dead body, attending a funeral, or visiting a Jewish cemetery,

7. After taking a bath or shower, or leaving a bathhouse.

V. PROCEDURE FOR WASHING NETILAS YODAYIM

Important—The following rules apply to the *morning* washing only. (In the other instances listed above, no *Brocho* is made.) In the cases of leaving the toilet, touching one's shoes or covered parts of the body, or scratching hair, there is no need to wash three times, but the amount of water needed is the same as in the morning.

1. The hands should be washed alternately, three times each, starting with the right hand.

2. If one washes each hand four times, then he does not have to dry his hands as carefully as he would after washing three times. The fourth washing completely removes the last vestiges of *Tumah* (impurity) that remain on the hands.

3. After washing, one should recite the *Brocho, "Al Netilas Yodayim."*

4. A person must wash his face after washing *Netilas Yodayim.* If he washed each hand four times, he may wash his face immediately. If he washed only three times, he should wipe his hands first (in order to remove the last vestiges of *Tumah*) and then wash his face and rinse his mouth.

every occasion. Those *Tefillos* recited most often, *Shacharis* (morning), *Mincha* (afternoon), and *Ma'ariv* (evening), are found at the beginning of the *Siddur.* They are followed by the services for *Shabbos* and *Yom Tov.* The rest of the *Siddur* is devoted to prayers recited on special occasions: e.g., *Hallel*—a service of praise and thanksgiving, recited on *Yom Tov, Rosh Chodesh* and *Chanukah; Birchos Hamazon* (Grace After Meals); prayers before going to bed; and part of the services recited on *Yom Tov* and the *Yomim Noraim* (High Holidays).

The *Siddur* is composed of many different categories of prayers:

(1) PRAISE—We praise *Hashem* as the Creator of heaven and earth and declare that His Holiness and His Presence exist in all parts of the universe. We declare the power of *Hashem* to do whatever He wills, and we testify to His loving kindness.

(2) THANKSGIVING—Jews all over the world recite prayers of thanksgiving every day. We thank *Hashem* for the blessings of life and for the blessings He grants us personally. We thank Him for giving us the Torah and providing us with food, clothing, shelter, and all the rest of our needs.

(3) REQUEST—Many people think that the only time it is necessary to pray to *Hashem* is when they want something special. This attitude is

VI. REASONS FOR NETILAS YODAYIM

There are four basic reasons for washing the hands upon awakening.

1) While sleeping, we might have touched those limbs that are normally covered during the day, thereby impurifying the hands and making one unfit for reciting *Hashem's* name.

2) When we awaken in the morning, we welcome our *Neshama* (soul) back into our bodies: in essence, we become a *Briah Chadasha*, a new creation.

3) Just as the *Kohein* washed his hands each morning before performing the *Avodah* (service) in the *Beis Hamikdosh* (Temple), so too, we wash our hands every morning before davening.

4) A general impurity *(Ruach Ro'oh)* covers one's hands and body during a night's sleep and this is removed by washing the hands.

VII. WHAT SHOULD ONE DO IF HE HAS NOT SLEPT DURING THE NIGHT

1. According to reason 1) above, it would not be necessary to wash, since one would have been conscious of his actions and would know whether or not he had touched any part of his body.

2. If, as the second reason indicates, he becomes a *Briah Chadasha*, regardless of whether or not he has slept at night, he would have to wash.

Therefore, if one has not slept all night, he must still wash his hands,

wrong. We should not take our daily well-being for granted. Without *Hashem's* constant kindness, we could not survive for a moment. Therefore, our requests and prayers are always needed for peace throughout the world, especially for *"Shalom Al Yisroel."* We ask Him to teach us to care for our fellow men and to bless us with a happy and healthy life, one devoted to Torah and Jewish ideals. We ask for the privilege of witnessing the return of all Jews to *Eretz Yisroel,* the coming of the *Moshiach,* and the rebuilding of the *Bais Hamikdosh.*

There is no better means of approaching Hashem than through prayer, for in the very hour that Israel prays and praises Hashem, lifting their eyes and hearts toward Heaven, the Holy one, Blessed be He looks down upon them, embraces them, and is overjoyed to hear their voices. (Koheles)

The effect of prayer on the human spirit is like that of fire on coals. Just as the flame clothes the black sooty clod in a garment of fire and releases the heat imprisoned therein, so does prayer clothe a man in a garment of holiness, evoking the light and fire implanted within him by His Maker, illuminating his whole being and uniting the World Above with that Below. (Zohar)

THE ULTIMATE PRAYER

It was 6:30 in the evening and the Shul was already filled to capacity. Old

but he should not say the *Brocho, "Al Netilas Yodayim,"* until after he has gone to the bathroom. This *Brocho* is followed by *"Asher Yotzar."*

3. If one wakes up in the middle of the night, washes *Netilas Yodayim,* and then remains awake, it is questionable whether or not he should wash again when daybreak comes. In this case, he should go to the toilet and wash *Netilas Yodayim* prior to reciting *"Al Netilas Yodayim"* and *"Asher Yotzar."* However, if he returns to sleep while it was still dark, he should wash in the regular manner when morning comes.

4. After awakening, one should wash *Netilas Yodayim* generally before going to the bathroom unless he feels the need, in which case he should delay washing until afterwards. In either case, one recites the *Brocho* of *"Al Netilas Yodayim"* followed by *"Asher Yotzar."*

VIII. ASHER YOTZAR

1. The *Brocho* of *"Asher Yotzar"* (thanking *Hashem* for the bodily process) is said after going to the bathroom.

2. If one forgot to say this *Brocho,* he may recite it when he remembers, even if he did not use the bathroom again at that time.

3. If he did use the bathroom again, the *"Asher Yotzar"* he recites suffices for both times. He need not recite it twice.

4. It is not necessary to dry one's hands after reciting *"Asher Yotzar."* (However, it *is* necessary when washing for bread.)

---

men with flowing white beards, young children in their *Yom Tov* finery—all had wished to be on time for the start of the *Yom Tov davening.* Soon the town's spiritual leader, Reb Levi Yitzchok, would enter and then the services would begin.

Reb Levi Yitzchok had been the town's leader for over 30 years. He was recognized far and wide as a great Torah scholar and a man of impeccable righteousness. People from all over the world would come to the town, seeking Reb Levi Yitzchok's blessings and advice.

The wise men of the town would often say that there was much more to Reb Levi Yitzchok than most people realized. They said that he spent hours on end in seclusion, delving into the secrets of the Torah. They spoke of him as an angel, clothed in human features.

It was 6:45. The davening was already five minutes late in starting. Reb Levi Yitzchok was usually on time. Well, the people thought, he is probably preparing his mind and soul for the special *Yom Tov* prayers. He certainly wouldn't keep the congregation waiting too long; he never did. It became 7:15. Some people were getting restless. It certainly was very unlike Reb Levi Yitzchok to keep the people waiting. Was something wrong? They had someone check to see if Reb Levi Yitzchok was in good health. The custodian ran to Reb Levi Yitzchok's room and quietly peeked through the keyhole. There sat Reb Levi Yitzchok,

IX. DRESSING IN THE MORNING

1. One should not walk around at home without being dressed, for he is conducting himself immodestly in the presence of Hashem.

2. One should be careful to don his *Yarmulke (Kipah)* and *Tzitzis* immediately upon arising in the morning. The wearing of *Tzitzis* is a Torah commandment designed to remind one of *Hashem's Mitzvos* while the *Yarmulke* alerts one to behave respectfully and humbly in *Hashem's* presence.

One should not walk further than four *Amos* (approx. 7 feet) when bareheaded, unless he is swimming or bathing. In circumstances where one finds it difficult to wear a Yarmulke (in some business office) one can substitute a toupee; however, it is preferable to wear a Yarmulke, since people might suspect he is going bareheaded.

Although a straw hat or a knitted *Yarmulke* may have many small holes, they are still considered acceptable head coverings.

3. One should put on one's right shoe first but tie the laces of the left shoe first.

The reason we put on the right shoe before the left is because the Torah considers the right side of the body to be more important than the left. For example, newly consecrated priests had the blood of the sacrificial ram sprinkled on "the thumb of the right hand and the toe of the right foot." (*Vayikroh* 8:23). However, when one ties a knot, the left takes precedence over the right, since the knot of the *Tefillin* is usually tied on the left hand.

wrapped in his *tallis,* swaying slowly to and fro. He seemed to be healthy. What could be keeping him? Perhaps he had become so engrossed in his preparations that he had lost track of time. Should they go in and remind him that everyone was waiting? Was there a volunteer who dared enter Reb Levi Yitzchok's room? The people decided to wait a few more minutes.

It was now 7:35. Something must be wrong. Avrohom the baker volunteered. He would knock on the door and ask the Rabbi what was the matter. He began to make his way towards Reb Levi Yitzchok's room. Suddenly, there was a hush in the Shul. Reb Levi Yitzchok was coming! The people

returned to their seats and waited for Reb Levi Yitzchok to give some sort of indication as to what had delayed him. To everyone's surprise, he said nothing. He simply nodded his head for the services to start.

After the prayers were concluded the people lined up to wish Reb Levi Yitzchok a good *Yom Tov.* Suddenly, Reb Levi Yitzchok began to make his way through the crowd and moved slowly towards the *Aron Kodesh.* He kissed the curtain which covered the Aron and then turned towards the congregation, ready to speak. A hush fell over the crowd.

"A good *Yom Tov,* my very dear friends. I do not want to keep you any

תפלה
Tefillah

INTRODUCTION—TEFILLAH

It is a positive commandment to pray every day to G-d, as it says (Devorim 6) "You should serve Him." From Chazal (Taanis 6), we learn that service is rendered to G-d through prayer as it says (Devorim 11) "To serve with all your heart." How does one serve with his heart? Through prayer. (Taanis 2)

"With my voice I cry unto the L-rd; with my voice I make supplication unto the L-rd, I pour out my request before Him. I declare before Him my trouble." (Tehillim, 142: 1, 3)

"Now there is no Novi, no Kehuna, no sacrifice, no temple who will forgive us. We have only prayer alone." (Medrash Tanchuma, Parshas Vayishlach)

HILCHOS TEFILLAH

1. One should not eat or do any work before *Tefillah*. He should not greet his friend with *Sholom Aleichem*.

2. He must daven in a place where he will be free of distractions and will

longer, but please allow me just a few minutes to explain my delay tonight. Actually, I was prepared to leave my room at 6:20. However, it was revealed to me from Heaven that it was important that our *davening* be delayed. You see, there is a man in this town who did not come to Shul tonight. He was never taught how to read and so he was ashamed to come here. But this man is a very pious, sincere Jew and in G-d's eyes he is a great man. Tonight, this man sat in his room and cried. He said to G-d, "Hashem, I do not know how to read. I cannot pray as everyone else does. Hashem, there

is one thing that I do know. I know the *Aleph-Bais*, all 22 letters. Let the *Aleph-Bais* be my prayer tonight."

Reb Levi Yitzchok continued. "The man stood up and slowly uttered each letter of the *Aleph-Bais*—one by one. With each letter, the man's voice rose. He cried tears of joy as he expressed his love for *Hashem* by simply repeating the Hebrew alphabet over and over again.

"The Angels of Prayer realized how precious this man's prayers were, and decided to offer some help. They took the letters that this man spoke and arranged them so that they formed

be able to concentrate on his prayer. He should not daven holding something in his hand, or standing in a place where he may be interrupted, or where there is fear of falling.

3. One should daven with a *Minyan* in a Shul. If he cannot find such a place with both conditions, he should daven with a *Minyan*, even though it is not in a Shul. If this is not possible, he should daven in Shul even without a *Minyan*. If this is also not possible he should daven in a room without distractions, facing East. If one cannot daven indoors, he should find a sheltered place (e.g.; a tree) and face East.

4. It is a *Mitzvah* to hurry to daven. In addition, one should try to be among the first ten to enter the Shul.

5. A person should have a set place *(Makom Kavoah)* for davening. Preferably, he should daven where he learns.

6. He should dress appropriately for *Tefillah*, as he is speaking to *Hashem*. It is advisable that if possible, one wear a hat, jacket and belt. This shows a special respect.

7. A person should go to the bathroom before he goes to Shul.

I. BROCHOS (Blessings)

1. *Brochos* are prayers in which we may either praise, thank or make requests to *Hashem*. Some prayers express thanks for the sustenance He provides every day. Some praise Him for the opportunity to perform *Mitzvos*, while others serve as expressions of celebration on various special occasions.

words of prayers. Then they placed the words before the throne of Hashem."

"The task the angels were performing was so special, that they asked for our prayers to be delayed until this man had completed his praying."

"Let us learn something from this story," Reb Levi Yitzchok concluded. "One might be the simplest of men, but if one is sincere and tries to serve *Hashem* as best as he can, He will always listen to that man's prayers. We need not search for glory and honor in this world. It is he who is most humble and honest that is accorded the most honor in Heaven."

A Chassid once complained to the Kotzker Rebbe, ZTL that he found it most difficult to earn a living. The *Rebbe* counseled him to pray to *Hashem* to have mercy upon him. The *Chassid* declared that he didn't think that his own prayer would help with the Almighty.

The *Rebbe* responded, "If that is your feeling, then you have a much greater problem than just the lack of a livelihood. You should feel more upset that you do not know how to express your innermost feelings to the *Ribono Shel Olam*."

We have no doubt that *Hashem* hears our prayers. Haven't Jews been praying for 4,000 years? Thousands throughout the ages have testified that

2. One should recite 100 *Brochos* each day. This practice was initiated by *Dovid Hamelech* (King David) following the onset of a plague that daily took the lives of 100 Jews. After the adoption of this practice, the plague ceased.

3. An unlearned person who cannot recite a *Brocho*, may have someone else say it in his presence on his behalf, but in most cases, it is best to recite the *Brocho* oneself, word by word.

4. After hearing a *Brocho*, one should respond *"Omein"* (Amen). Most authorities hold that this also applies when one has heard a *Brocho* with the help of a hearing aid.

II. BIRCHOS HATORAH (Blessings On The Torah)

1. One must recite *Birchos HaTorah* before learning Torah. Therefore, these *Brochos* are said at the beginning of the day.

2. In order to ensure that the *Birchos HaTorah* not be in vain *(L'Vatoloh)*, one should be certain to learn Torah during the day. It is for this reason that immediately following *Birchos HaTorah*, we say *Birchos Kohanim* (which is from the Torah) and *"Eilu Devorim"* (which is from the *Mishnayos*). However, even if one did not learn or say this immediately after *Birchas Hatorah*, the *Brocho* is still valid, since living as a Jew is considered Torah. (Rav Moshe Feinstein, Shlita).

---

prayer helped where everything else failed. Throughout *T'nach* we find numerous recorded instances where *Hashem* responded to the *Tefillos* of *Klal Yisroel* instantly. *Dovid HaMelech* says in *Tehillim*, (145:18) *"Korov Hashem L'Chol Kor'Ov L'Chol Asher Yikro'u'hu B'Emes"*; "Hashem is near to all who call upon Him, to all who call upon Him in truth."

Rabbi Zeira said: "The first time a man has a visitor, he seats him on the couch; the second time—on the chair; the third—on the bench; the fourth time he already grumbles, 'How much longer is he going to disturb me?' "

But the *Ribono Shel Olam* grows more satisfied the more His children, *Bnai Yisroel*, appeal to Him through prayer.

"When the Jews go to Shul and Beis Medrash *and say "the great*

Name should be blessed," G-d shakes His head and says, *"Happy is the King that His people praise Him in His house like this. Woe to the father who sent His children away and woe to the children who were sent away by the father."* (Brochos 3)

GREATNESS HAS MANY LEVELS

A poor ignorant Jewish youth spent his days as a simple shepherd. He had not received any schooling and his talents seemed limited to one ability. He could be heard whistling clear across the countryside. This held him in good stead when he was summoning his sheep and his family praised him for it.

However, he felt dissatisfied with his lot. He sensed that there was more to life than just herding sheep. There-

3. If one did not sleep at night, it is questionable whether he should say the *Birchos HaTorah.* Therefore, he should fulfill his obligation to recite these *Brochos* by asking someone else to be *Motzee* him (include him in the *Brocho* while saying them aloud).

4. Women can also say *Birchos HaTorah* if they learn Torah. Even though they are not obligated to learn Torah in the same manner as men, nevertheless, they must know the parts of the Torah that have practical applications for them.

5. If one is unsure as to whether or not he has recited the *Birchos HaTorah,* he should repeat only the *Brocho* of *"Asher Bochar Banu."* If one realizes he neglected to say these *Brochos* before reciting *"Ahavah Rabbah"* (the *Brocho* before *Shema*), he should not go back and recite the *Birchas HaTorah.* Rather, someone else should be *motzee* him; or, if this is not possible, then *"Ahavah Rabbah"* can be considered a substitute for the *Birchas HaTorah* if he learns Torah immediately after the *Tefillah.*

6. One should not answer *Omein* after *"La'asok B'Divrei Sorah,"* because the *Brocho* does not conclude until *"Hamelamed Torah L'Amo Yisroel."*

III. BIRCHOS HASHACHAR (Morning Blessings)

1. The *Birchos HaShachar* are recited in the morning immediately after *Birchos HaTorah.* These Brochos thank Hashem in a systematic

fore, he let his curiosity roam and began investigating the world around him. One of his expeditions took him to a small hut, whose walls bore a plaque with strange-looking writings. This caught his attention and he decided to enter the building. Inside, he found a group of men standing and chanting reverently in the direction of a small ark. The devotion of the men entranced him. He watched as they prayed and wished that he, too, could join in their chanting. But he had never learned the language they were speaking, and he found it impossible to follow them. Finally, his yearnings to participate made him act. He rushed up to the front of the building, faced the ark, and let out an ear-piercing whistle.

The members of the congregation turned to the youth with angry expressions on their faces. Was he trying to mock their worship of the L-rd? But the Rabbi of the shul calmed them by saying, "The boy meant no harm. He simply wanted to join us in prayer, but he didn't know how. The only way he could express his emotions was through whistling, and this is what he did. So please accept this as his form of worship, and realize that he was using his greatest talent in the service of Hashem."

The congregation greeted the youth as one of their own and they came to admire him greatly. He was determined to serve Hashem as best he could, and he successfully achieved

fashion for enabling us to do various things in the morning that we so often take for granted.

2. A *Ger* (convert to Judaism) should say the blessings of *"Shelo Osani Eved"* (Who did not make me a servant) and *"Shelo Osani Ishah"* (Who did not make me a woman) but not the blessing of *"Shelo Osani Goy"* (Who did not make me a gentile).

3. The blessing of *"Shelo Osani Ishah"* is recited by men only. This blessing is not meant to degrade or downplay the role of women in Jewish life, but rather refers to the fact that men are obligated to perform more *Mitzvos* than women. Women say the blessing of *"She'Osani Kirtzono"* (Who made me as He willed) instead of *"Shelo Osani Ishah."*

4. If one accidentally recited the blessing of *"Shelo Osani Ishah"* before the blessing of *"Shelo Osani Goy,"* it is questionable as to whether he should still say *"Shelo Osani Goy."* He should, therefore, be *yotzai* with someone else's blessings. The same applies to one who mistakenly said *"Zokaif Kefufim"* before *"Matir Assurim."*

5. A blind person must say the blessing of *"Pokeiach Ivrim"* (who gives sight to the blind) because he is aided by those who can see.

6. If one was awake all night, he cannot say the blessings of *"Elokai Neshomo"* and *"HaMa'avir Shainah"* (who removes sleep) through *"HaGomel Chassodim Tovim L'Amo Yisroel."* Therefore he should be *yotzai* with somebody else.

---

his own level of greatness.

A little prayer with devotion is better than a lot without.

* * * * *

Rabbi Levi Yitzchok of Berditchov once walked into a Shul during *Shmoneh Esrei* where he stood and observed the people. He then walked over to a group of his *Chassidim* in the Shul after they had finished *davening*, and greeted them with the words, *"Sholom Aleichem* (Welcome)." They were most surprised at this unexpected salute since they hadn't been away.

Seeing the look of surprise on their faces, the Berditchever explained as follows: "I could tell from the look on your faces while reciting *'Shmoneh Esrei'* that you didn't have in mind the

meaning of the words of the prayers you were saying. Instead, you were thinking about the grain market in Odessa or the wool market in Lodz. Now that you have returned from such a long trip, it's appropriate for me to extend to you a *'Sholom Aleichem—* Welcome home!' "

THE PRAYER OF NAKDIMON BEN GURION

In the time of the *Bais Hamikdosh*, the *Bnai Yisroel* were *oleh regel* (made pilgrimages to Yerusholayim) three times a year. It happened one year that there was a drought because no rain had fallen for a long time. (*Taanis* 19b)

At that time, there lived in Yerusholayim a wealthy man, Nakdimon ben

7. One should respond *Omein* to every blessing recited by the *Chazan*. When listening to the *Brocho* of *"Hama'avir Sheinah"* one should not answer *Omain* after the word *"Mei'Af'Apai"* as the *Brocho* concludes with *"HaGomel Chassodim Tovim L'Amo Yisroel."*

IV. LAWS OF P'SUKEI D'ZIMRAH

A. BORUCH SHE'AMAR

1. The prayers from *Boruch She'amar* to *Borchu* are called *P'sukei D'zimrah*. One should not talk, even in Hebrew, during these prayers.

2. One is allowed, however, to answer *Omein* after the Chazan's completion of *Boruch She'amar* provided he has completed the *Boruch She'amar* before the Chazan. A man should kiss his *Tzitsis* at the conclusion of the *Brocho*.

3. An orphan is permitted to say *Kaddish* even if he is in the middle of saying *P'sukei D'zimrah* and the rest of the congregation is up to the *Kaddish*.

4. When saying *Hodu,* one should pause briefly between the words *"Elilim"* and *"Va'Hashem Shomayim Osoh,"* as if to separate the mention of G-d's name from that of false deities.

5. *Mizmor L'Sodah* is not said on *Shabbos, Yom Tov, Erev Pesach, Chol Ha'Moed Pesach* and *Erev Yom Kippur* because on these days the *Korbon Todah* (offering of thanks) could not be brought.

Gurion, who felt he must do something for his fellow Jews who showed such sacrifice by coming to Yerusholayim three times a year. Nakdimon went to the Governor of Yerusholayim and asked him to lend him twelve reservoirs of water so that the people should have enough to drink. The agreement was that Nakdimon would repay him an equal amount of water within a given time. If he missed the deadline, he would have to pay an additional twelve sacks of silver.

When the day arrived on which Nakdimon was supposed to return the water, it still had not rained. When the Governor demanded what was due him, Nakdimon replied, "The day isn't over yet."

The Governor laughed and said, "If it has not rained by now, do you expect to fill up twelve reservoirs by the end of the day?" The Governor walked away happily to the baths, thinking he had already won the money, while Nakdimon went to Shul, wrapped himself in his *tallis*, and began to pray to *Hashem*.

"L-rd of the Universe," he said, "you know that what I did was not for the sake of my honor but for Your honor, that Your children who come *oleh regal* should have water to drink."

No sooner had he finished his prayer than *Hashem* answered him. Dark clouds covered the sky and a heavy rain poured down, quickly filling the reservoirs to overflowing.

As the Governor came out of the baths, he met Nakdimon coming out

6. The most important passage in *Ashrei* is *"Poseiach Es Yodecho."* When saying this, one should concentrate on the thought that it is *Hashem* Who supplies all of our needs.

7. One should arrive on time to pray with the *Minyan*. If he davens more slowly than the other congregants, then he should begin earlier so that he can say *Shmoneh Esrei* with a *Minyan*.

8. If one arrives late to *Shul* and is almost certain that he will not be able to daven *Shmoneh Esrei* with the *Minyan*, he should omit certain *Tefillos* in order to catch up to the *Brochos* of *Krias Shema*. The following prayers must always be said first (even if it means not saying *Shmoneh Esrei* together with the *Tzeebur* (congregation)). *Birchos HaShachar, Boruch She'Amar, Ashrei,* and *Yishtabach.* (On Shabbos, *Nishmas* is added to this group.)

9. The prayers with the next highest priority are the *Hallelukoh's* (first *"Hallelukoh Hallelu Kail B'Kodshoh,"* then, *"Hallelukoh Hallelu Es Hashem Min HaShomayim,"* then the rest of the *Hallelukoh's*). The prayers with the next level of priority are *Vayivoreich Dovid* and *Hodu* till the words of *Romemu.*

10. According to Rav Moshe Feinstein, *Shlita,* if someone already said the *Hallelukohs* and now realizes that he still has more time to say additional *Tefillos,* he can say *Hodu* and *Vayevoreich Dovid,* even if they are now not in the proper order.

of the synagogue, and said to him: "I know very well that G-d sent this heavy rain for your sake. Nevertheless, you still owe me my money, for the sun had already set when it rained."

Nakdimon went back to the Shul, put on his *tallis* and prayed to *Hashem:* "L-rd of the Universe, just as You have performed a miracle for me by sending the rain, please perform another by causing the sun to reappear." Immediately a wind arose, the clouds scattered, and the sun shone again.

Chazal tell us (*Taanis* 20) that for the sake of three men the sun stood still: (1) Moshe Rabbeinu, when he defeated Amalek, (2) Yehoshua, for whom the sun stood still when he fought the kings in Givah, and (3)

Nakdimon ben Gurion.

"G-d said to Dovid, "It is better to me one prayer that you stand and pray for men, than one thousand sacrifices that Solomon will bring for me." (Medrash Tanchuma Shabbos 30)

THE PRAYER OF RABBI CHANINA

When his son fell seriously ill, Rabban Gamliel (the *Nasi*) sent two Sages to Rabbi Chanina ben Dosa to pray for his recovery. As soon as Rabbi Chanina spoke with the two Sages, he quickly ran up to the loft of his house and prayed with great *kavonoh* (feeling) that the fever should subside and the boy recover. When he came back down, he said to them, "Go in peace, for the fever has left the boy."

11. These laws of leaving out *Tefillos* and saying them later apply only if one is sure he can catch up to the congregation *(Tzeebur)*. If he can't catch up in time, he should just daven in the order of the *Siddur*. Furthermore, the above laws do not apply to one who is habitually late, who must pray in the order of the *Siddur*.

12. One is permitted to answer *Omein* to *Kaddish*, *Borchu*, and *Kedusha*.

B. YISHTABACH AND BORCHU

1. *Yishtabach* is considered part of a series of *Brochos* with *Boruch She'Amar*, and, therefore, does not begin with a *Brocho*.

2. One can answer *Omein* if he finishes *Yishtabach* with the Chazan.

3. We bow at the beginning of *Borchu*.

4. One is not permitted to talk after *Yishtabach*. No one should call out the page number of the prayer being recited from this point on, unless he is not praying together with the congregation.

C. KADDISH

1. The *Kaddish* is recited only if a *Minyan* (quorum of 10 adult males) is present. (Any member of a *Minyan* of ten who leaves before the conclusion of the *davening* is severely condemned.) If the congregation is up to *Chazoras Ha'Shatz*, and one of the 10 men left, they may continue. The

---

The two were astounded. "But how do you know that? Who told you?"

Rabbi Chanina replied: "I am neither a prophet nor the son of a prophet, but I have a tradition from my grandfather that if a prayer runs smoothly, then it is a sign that it has been heard. My prayer just now ran smoothly, without any hindrance. I am, therefore, sure it was heard."

The two men noted down the time that Rabbi Chanina informed them of the patient's recovery. When they returned to Rabban Gamliel, they told him the exact time. Rabban Gamliel assured them that this was the very time when the fever left his son. *(Brochos 34)*

"Prayer reunites the afflicted with their Father in Heaven."

The Six Day War of 1967 was at its height, and Israeli tanks were pouring into the Sinai, on their way to the Suez Canal. One such tank was manned by three young Israelis, all observant Jews. As they plowed ahead, one suggested that they say *Tehillim*, to ask G-d for their safety. As he was about to do so, his companions noticed a group of tanks approaching straight towards them. They were enemy tanks!

Immediately, they positioned the tank into firing position. It was then that one of the soldiers made a horrifying discovery. The tank's firing mechanism was jammed. The huge guns would not work. And yet, the enemy tanks kept rolling onward, ever closer. What could they do?

"There is only one thing we can

reduced congregation may also say the *Kaddish Sholem* (complete *Kaddish*) after *U'Vo L'Tzion*, but none of the other prayers that require a *Minyan*.

2. Upon hearing *Kaddish* one should remain quiet and answer *Omein* at the proper moments. It is also best for one to stand during its recitation.

3. One should pause slightly between the words *"Omein"* and *"Yehai Sh'mai Rabboh."* However, there should be no pause between the words, *"Yehai Sh'mai Rabboh"* and *"Mevorach."* The whole sentence should be said loudly and clearly.

4. Responding to *Kaddish* takes precedence over responding to *Kedusha*. However, if one has already begun responding to *Kedusha* said by one *Minyan*, he should not stop to respond to *Kaddish* said by another.

5. If one enters the Shul while the congregation is saying *"Omein, Yehai Sh'mai Rabboh,"* he should respond along with them even though he didn't hear the beginning of *Kaddish*.

6. During the recitation of the *Kaddish*, one bows by *Yisgadel*, *Yehai Sh'mai*, *Yisborach*, *Brichu*, and *Ve'imru Omein*, the person takes three steps back and ends by saying the phrase that begins *"Oseh Sholom,"* bowing three times, left, (at *"Oseh Sholom Bimromav"*), right (at *"Oseh Sholom Oleinu"*), and forward (at *"Al Kol Yisroel Omein"*).

resort to at a time like this." said the first man, and he opened the *Tehillim* and began reciting it with great feeling.

Then, to his companions' astonishment, they noticed the enemy tanks suddenly halt and raise white flags of surrender. Unbelieving, they watched as the tank doors opened, and several soldiers emerged. "They are not Arabs!" the men exclaimed. "They are Israelis!"

When the Israelis reached them, they explained the strange situation. They had captured the still-functioning Arab tanks in battle, and were now bringing them back to the central Israeli command. They had hoped that no Israelis would mistake them for the enemy, and had watched nervously as this particular tank had gone into firing position. But then, miraculously, the guns had not fired. Both groups of soldiers had been saved— apparently through Divine deliverance, helped by the power of prayer.

THE WASTED REQUEST

If we consider the matter honestly, we will find that we concentrate most in our prayers when we ask for our own physical well-being. However, when it comes to prayer about other matters—such as repentance and spiritual well-being, then only a select, precious few pour out their wishes from the depth of their heart.

A king once came to inspect a military camp in his country. The soldiers stood at attention while the king moved about examining them carefully. Needless to say, everyone strove

D. SH'LIACH TZEEBUR (CHAZAN)

1. One who is selected as a *Sh'liach Tzeebur* (Chazan) must be a *Shomer Shabbos*, a *Ben Torah*, and a person who avoids arguments. He should have a pleasant voice and should enunciate the words clearly and correctly without lengthening the *davening* excessively.

2. One who has been asked to be the *Sh'liach Tzeebur*, should not refuse more than twice; then he should accept and proceed to the *Omud* (place from which the *Chazan* prays) without hesitation.

V. LAWS OF KRIAS SHEMA IN THE MORNING

1. The very earliest time one may say *Krias Shema* in the morning, and then only in extenuating circumstances, is from *Alos HaShachar* (the time the first rays of light appear on the eastern horizon, which is approx. 72 minutes before sunrise.) The Mogen Avraham measured the day as the period between *Alos Hashachar* and *Tzais HaKochavim* (the appearance of three stars), thereby making for a longer day. It is best to read the *Shema* after there is enough daylight to recognize someone standing four cubits away. Opinions on this time period vary from 35 to 60 minutes before sunrise and one should consult a Rav on this matter.

2. It is preferable to say *Shema* immediately before *Neitz Hachama* (sunrise) so that one can recite the *Shmoneh Esrei* precisely at sunrise. This is called *Tefilas Kavosiken*. One fulfills the obligation to say *Krias*

to look his very best and make a good impression; and the king was pleased at the fine sight they made. Said he:

"You all look very good to me, and I am pleased indeed at what I have seen of you. Therefore, I grant you the right to come forward and ask any favor you wish, within reason, and it will be granted."

At that, one soldier sprang forward: "Your Majesty, I have something to request."

"Yes?" said the king, "What is your request?"

"I wish, Your Majesty, to order that my daily rations of food are to be given to me regularly, every day without fail."

Back in the barracks the man's fellow-soldiers poured out their scorn and contempt on his head: "You perfect idiot! For this you had to go and trouble the king with a special request? As long as you'll do your army duty faithfully and they keep you in the armed forces, you get your meals regularly in any case, automatically. You even get clothing and anything else you need. The king's treasury pays for it, for every soldier in the army. What lunacy it is to go and ask the king for regular meals, when he was in a particularly cheerful mood, ready to grant us special favors. Why didn't you ask for something really special instead?"

That is exactly what we are like. We do not understand that the main request we must make during *Tefillah* has to be the ability to become good, devout, observant Jews. We must

Shema in its proper time by saying it within a quarter of the day. The Vilna Gaon measured the day as the period between sunrise *(Neitz Hachamah)* and sunset *(Shkias Hachamah)*. If one was unable to do this, he should still recite *Shema* afterwards up to a third of the day (or noon, according to some), and thereby at least receive credit for learning Torah.

3. One should not stay up all night learning if that will cause him to get up late the next morning and miss the deadline for *Shema*.

4. Ordinarily, the *Tefillin* and/or *Tallis* should be donned before saying *Shema*. If one does not have *Tallis* and *Tefillin*, and will miss the time limit for *Shema* if he waits for them, he should say *Shema* without them.

A. THE BROCHOS BEFORE SHEMA

1. The Brochos before *Shema* include *"Yotzer Ohr"* and *"Ha'Bocheir B'Amo Yisroel B'Ahava."* One should try to recite these *Brochos* while sitting.

2. One should be careful to separate the words *"Yotzer"* and *"Ohr"* so that they do not sound like one word.

3. When saying the words *"Yotzer Ohr,"* one should touch his *Tefillin Shel Yad,* and when saying *"U'Vorei Choshech,"* he should do the same to his *Tefillin Shel Rosh.*

pray and implore Heaven's help to be able to be loyal soldiers, serving our blessed Maker in love and devotion. Then we will automatically be entitled to receive our "rations" of daily food, our clothing and all our needs out of the "royal treasury" of Divine Providence, as "regulars" in the "service" of the supreme King of Kings, the Holy One, blessed is He.

* * * * *

A pious man was travelling along the road when dusk fell. He then stopped at the edge of the road in order to pray. While he was in the middle of the *Shmoneh Esrei*, an officer approached him and asked what he was doing. The officer looked very important, but the Jew did not respond, and simply continued praying. After he had finished, the officer

shouted at him angrily, "You fool! Why didn't you answer me on the spot? I could have killed you for your insolence!"

The Jew replied, "Permit me to explain my behavior. If you were standing before a King, would you have interrupted your speech to greet a friend?"

"Of course not," said the officer.

"Then you can certainly understand what I did. If you'd be afraid of interrupting your speech to a mere mortal King, then how much more so should I be afraid of interrupting my prayers to the eternal King of Kings. When I speak to G-d, I have to devote all my concentration to this. How, then, could I have interrupted my prayers to answer you?" (*Brochos* 32)

(The man knew that he would not

4. The sentence beginning, *"Kodosh Kodosh Kodosh"* should be said out loud with the congregation. The same goes for the words *"Boruch K'Vod Hashem Mim'Komo."*

5. One should answer *Omein* after the Chazan completes *Yotzer Ha'Meoros.* However, if he has not yet completed the *Brocho* or even if he completes it simultaneously with the *Sh'liach Tzeebur,* he does not answer *Omein.*

6. If one had previously said *Shema* without the *Brochos,* he repeats *Shema* with them.

7. If an individual praying alone mistakenly said only one of the *Brochos,* he has fulfilled his obligation, but should say the omitted *Brocho* after *Shmoneh Esrei.*

8. A blind person can say *Yotzer Ha'Meoros* even though he cannot see the light referred to in the prayer, since he is aided by those who can see.

9. One should take out all four *Tzitzis* during the *Brocho* of *Ha'Bocher B'Amo Yisroel B'Ahava.*

B. SHEMA YISROEL

1. It is preferable to say *Shema* while seated. One must not stand up in

be harmed if he did not respond. If, however, there is a question of life or death, a person should interrupt his prayers to respond.)

"A person who davens must picture himself as if G-d is in front of him as it says, "I put G-d always in front of me." (Sanhedrin 22)

WORDS WITHOUT THOUGHT

"All employees report to the manager's office."

The call went out over the factory's public address system and soon all the workers were assembled before the manager. This procedure had been going on each day for several weeks, ever since the company owner had left the country on an important business trip. He had always directed the factory's operations personally, but now he had appointed a manager to oversee

the work of his employees and to insure that everything functioned smoothly during his absence.

Now all of these employees listened, bored, as the manager read aloud the instructions left behind by the boss. He carefully pronounced each word just as the owner had ordered and did a masterful job of delivering the instructions.

When the boss returned he was shocked to see the condition of his factory. Machines needed repairs and workers stood around idle. He angrily called in the manager and asked him for an explanation.

"Did you follow the instructions I left behind with you?"

"Why, of course," the manager defended himself. "I read them to all of the workers every day while you were gone."

the middle of *Shema*. If one is standing during *Shema*, he should remain in one spot. If one is walking, he should stop and stand in one spot when he gets to *Shema* and say it with *Kavono*.

2. Before saying *Shema Yisroel*, one should pause for a moment to contemplate what he will be saying.

3. One must say the first sentence of *Shema*, "SHEMA YISROEL HASHEM ELOKEINU HASHEM ECHOD" with deep concentration or else he has not fulfilled the *Mitzvah* properly.

4. When saying the first sentence of *Shema*, one should place his right hand over his eyes, to aid him in concentrating. One should also say this sentence out loud, and slightly elongate the end of the word, *"ECHOD."* While saying *Hashem's* name, he should keep in mind that *Hashem* was, is and always will be the Almighty Ruler of the world. While saying *"ECHOD,"* he should keep in mind that *Hashem* is One Who reigns over all four corners of the universe.

5. When saying the sentence of *Shema*, one should be careful to pause after every two words, to consider the meaning of his words.

6. The next sentence, *"Boruch Sheim K'Vod Malchuso L'Olom Vo'ed,"* should be said quietly, except on *Yom Kippur*, when it is said aloud.

7. One should pause briefly between the end of this sentence and the beginning of the passage beginning with *V'Ohavtoh*.

"Now I know why there is such a mess!" cried the boss. "You only read these instructions but you didn't bother to see that they were carried out. The lazy workers took advantage of your foolishness and almost ruined my entire business. Do you think that I left behind these instructions only for reading? I gave them to you so that you know how to run the factory in my absence. Just reading them has not achieved this goal."

Someone who reads the *Shema* daily without any thought to the words he is saying is like our silly manager.

The purpose of *Krias Shema* is not just to read the words, but to feel them with all of one's heart and soul. Only in this way can the important principles contained in these chapters become a vital part of our Torah lives.

DRAW THE BOW CLOSER

In speaking to Joseph, Yaakov said, "I have given you a greater portion than your brothers, a portion that I have taken from the *Emori* with my sword and my bow." *Rashi* explains that "with my sword" means "my wisdom," and "with my bow" means "my prayer."

The Kotzker Rebbe asks: "We can understand that 'my sword' can be used to describe wisdom. A swordsman must be very clever in trying to outwit his opponent; his mind must be quick and alert to ward off the piercing thrusts of the person that he is dueling with. "But, what does a bow and arrow have to do with prayer?" The Rebbe

8. *Shema* is composed of 245 words. Each word should be enunciated very clearly. When *Shema* is said by a congregation, the Chazan first says *"Hashem Elokeichem"* and then *"Hashem Elokeichem Emes"* out loud, to bring the word total to 248, corresponding to the number of *Mitzvos Assei.* A person who davens alone should begin the *Shema* with the preface, *"Kail Melech Ne'Emun"* to reach that total.

9. When saying the words, *"Asher Anochi M'Tzavcha Hayom,"* one should feel as though he had just received the *Mitzvos* that day.

10. When saying the words, *"U'Keshartom Le'os Al Yodecha,"* one should touch his *Tefillin Shel Yad.* When saying the words, *"Ve'Hoyu Letotofos Bein Einecha,"* he should touch his *Tefillin Shel Rosh.* And when saying the words, *"U'Re'Eesem Oso,"* he should take the *Tzitzis* in both hands, look at them, and then place them on his eyes.

11. If one reads the *p'sukim* (sentences) of *Shema* in the wrong order, he has not fulfilled the *Mitzvah.* However, if one says the three *parshios* (paragraphs) in the wrong order, he has fulfilled the *Mitzvah,* though one should not intentionally do so.

12. If one made an error while saying a *parsha* of *Shema* but does not know exactly where he made the error, he need not begin again from the start of the *Shema.* Rather, he should commence at the beginning of that specific *parsha.* If he knows the specific *posuk* containing the mistake, he need repeat only that *posuk* and continue from there.

answered: "The more you draw the bow closer to yourself, the higher and further away does the arrow fly. In the same way, the more you draw the prayers closer and deeper into your heart, the more *kavono* (sincerity) you daven with, the higher towards heaven will your prayers reach."

"Prayer without devotion is like a body without a soul." *(Yeshuos Meshicho)*

The Dubner Maggid once noticed that several people who resided in town had entered the Shul on *Rosh Hashono.* They had never shown their faces there during the rest of the year. Yet now they sat piously, wrapped in their *taleisim,* praying that Hashem should grant them a happy, prosperous new year.

That evening, when the Dubner Maggid ascended the pulpit to deliver his sermon, he told the congregants the following story:

"A merchant who had purchased all his goods on credit, suddenly lost everything in a fire. He was penniless and did not know how to tell his creditor that he could not repay him. A friend suggested that the best thing to do would be to tell his creditor the whole truth and perhaps he would extend him further credit, or even forgive the entire debt.

"The merchant listened to his friend's advice. He went to the manufacturer and told him of his misfortune. The manufacturer was touched by the honesty of the man and told him that not only would he forgive the

13. If one found it necessary to interrupt his recitation of *Shema* he need not commence again at the beginning, unless the interruption is equal to the time period necessary for him to say the entire *Shema*. There are many complicated laws involved here and a Rav should be consulted about them.

14. If one hears the congregation saying the *posuk* of *"Shema Yisroel,"* he should say it along with them even if he is elsewhere in his prayers. If, however, he is reciting the *Birchos Krias Shema* when the congregation says *Shema*, he should continue with his current prayer but make it appear as if he is saying *Shema*, by putting his right hand over his eyes. However, if one is in the middle of *Shmoneh Esrei*, he should just continue praying.

15. Women are not *halachically* required to recite the *Shema*, because saying it is a *Mitzvah* dependent on time, (a *Mitzvas Aseei She'Hazman G'romoh)*. However, since *Shema* refers to the acceptance of the Heavenly Kingdom and redemption from Egypt, and women are part of that, it is preferable for them to say *Shema*.

16. An *Onen* (mourner whose close relative has just died) is not required to say *Shema* or perform other *Mitzvos* until his relative has been buried. Similarly, one who is performing the *Mitzvah* of watching over the body of a dead person does not have to say *Shema*, even if he is not a relative of the dead person.

debt, but he was going to lend him an additional few thousand rubles to get started in business again.

"The merchant was jubilant and ran home to tell everyone of his good fortune. One of his listeners, a good-for-nothing fellow, decided that here was the chance to make some easy money. He went to the same manufacturer and, claiming extreme poverty, asked to be given a few thousand rubles. 'But why should I give you such an amount?' asked the wealthy man in amazement.

"Didn't you give my friend so much money? Am I worse than he?' "

"You fool" the rich man shouted. 'How can you compare yourself to the other? I've had business dealings with that man for years. Now when he was faced with a misfortune, I felt I had to help him. But who are you? I never saw you before and never had any business relations with you. How dare you come and ask me for money?' "

The Dubner Maggid concluded, "When a religious Jew who attends Shul all year round, does good deeds, and is in contact with *Hashem* constantly, commits a sin and repents, *Hashem* will forgive him. He should be treated with compassion and understanding. But when a total stranger, who has had no contact with G-d all year round, and has never entered a Shul, suddenly appears during the High Holidays and appeals to G-d to grant him long life, health, wealth and happiness—that, my friends, is indeed outright *Chutzpah!*"

17. One may not say *Shema* under any of the following conditions:
a) He is not dressed,
b) He is in front of someone who is not properly attired,
c) He can hear a woman singing,
d) He is close to a foul odor,
e) He is within four *amos* of dead person or at a cemetery.

18. If one must go to the bathroom during his recitation of *Shema*, he should do so between the words *"Hashem Elokeichem Emes"* and *"V'Yatziv V'nochon,"* or between the paragraphs of *Shema* if necessary.

19. One must be careful to enunciate the words clearly, and not run two words together.

C. HAFSAKOS (Interruptions) DURING SHEMA

1. If one finds it necessary to interrupt his recitation of *Shema* and the surrounding *Brochos,* he should do so between the *perokim* (sections) as follows:

a) between *"Yotzeir Ha'Meoros"* and *"Ahavah Rabbah";*
b) between *"Ha'Bocheir B'amo Yisroel B'Ahavah"* and *"Shema Yisroel";*
c) between *"Al Mezuzos Beisecha"* and *"V'Hoya Im Shomoa";*
d) between *"Kee'Mai Hashomayim Al Ho'Oretz"* and *"Vayomer."*

(During *Ma'ariv,* there is an additional place for interruption between the paragraphs of *"Go'al Yisroel"* and *"Hashkeeveinu."*)

"Resh Lakish said: 'Whosoever has a synagogue in his town and does not worship there is dubbed an evil neighbor. For it is said, 'Thus says the Lord, as for all My evil neighbors that touch the inheritance which I have caused my people Israel to inherit, behold I will pluck them up.'" (Brochos 8)

"Whoever sets a place for his prayer, G-d of Abraham will be on his side." (Brochos 6)

A king was once asked to decide which of two towns deserved a certain royal privilege. Both towns sent gifts to the king to win his favor. The members of the first town sent their gifts individually, at different times. As each gift arrived, the king examined it and usually managed to find fault with each one. The second town, however, sent their gifts in one shipment. When this bundle of gifts arrived, the king was at once impressed by the enormous number of gifts, and did not feel inclined to look at each gift individually. As would be expected, the second town won his favor.

In a similar vein, if each of us would pray separately, Hashem would examine each of us on an individual basis and would no doubt find us deficient. On the other hand, if we pray in a group, as part of a *Minyan,* then our combined prayers are conveyed to Hashem, and hopefully the merits of the entire group will outweigh the deficiencies of each individual in the group.

35

e) If absolutely necessary between *"Emes"* and *"V'yatziv"*.

2. One should not interrupt at all between the passages of *"Shema Yisroel"* and *"Boruch Sheim."*

3. If one is in the midst of *Shema* while the congregation is saying *Kedusha* or *Kaddish,* he should interrupt the *Shema* to answer only to the passages of *"Kodosh Kodosh Kodosh,"* *"Boruch K'vod,"* *"Borchu,"* *"Y'Hai Sh'mai Rabboh,"* *Omein* after *"Da'amiron Be'Olmo"* *"Hakel Hakodosh"* and *"Shomeiah Tefillah"* and the words *"Modim Anachnu Loch."* He should also answer to *Modim* during *Chazoras Ha'Shatz,* by bowing his head and saying the first three words of *Modim D'rabonon.* He should respond with *"Boruch Hashem Hamevorach Le'Olom Vo'Ed"* after both the *Borchu* before *Yotzer Ohr* and the *Borchu* of *Krias HaTorah.*

4. If one's *Tzitzis* and *Tefillin* became available only as he was reciting the *Shema,* he may interrupt between the *perokim* to say the *Brocho* on the *Tefillin* but not on the *Tzitzis.*

5. If one is called to the *Torah* during *Birchos Krias Shema,* he should attempt to continue davening until he gets to between the *perokim* before he goes up. However, as long as he is not in the middle of *Shema* and *Boruch Sheim,* he may say the *Brochos* but should not read along with the *Baal Kriah.*

One of the reasons why a *minyan* is necessary is because it is written: "Bless ye G-d in full assemblies" (*Psalms* 68:27). The total numerical value of the letters in *"Bemikhalos,"* the Hebrew word for "assemblies," is equal to that of *"Be'asoroh,"* the Hebrew for "with ten."

In order for a Jew not to be without Torah for three days in succession, we read portions of the Torah on *Shabbos,* Mondays and Thursdays. It is written: "And they went three days in the wilderness and found no water" (*Sh.* 15:22). From this verse we deduce the fact that three days must not go by without Torah (for the Torah is often referred to as "living waters"). (*Baba Kama* 82a)

The Rabbis rule that a portion of the Law to be read from by three individu-als must contain at least ten verses. This is so because anything less than ten verses would not be considered adequate. The portion containing the account of the Amalekite attack on the children of Israel, which is read at Purim time, is an exception to this rule for it contains only nine verses. (*Megillah* 21b)

The *Shulchan Oruch* writes: One should always make an effort to pray only in the synagogue even if there is no *minyan* present; even if one must pray by oneself, he should do so in the synagogue if at all possible. This is because the angels of destruction waylay those prayers which are not recited at a House of Sanctity. (*Oruch Chayim* 90:9)

The only way to ward off these angels of evil is to take unto oneself

6. One can interrupt his recitation of the *Shema*—even if he is in the middle of a paragraph—to read the *Torah,* if he is the only one available to do so. However, it is best if he makes the interruption between *perokim.*

7. One should not make any interruptions between the *Brocho* of *Go'al Yisroel* and the beginning of the *Shmoneh Esrei.* This applies to responding to *Kaddish* and *Kedusha* as well. Therefore, if one sees that he will probably reach Go'al Yisroel by the time the rest of the congregation has reached *Kaddish* or *Kedusha,* he should daven slowly so that he can respond with them when he is up to *"Shira Chadosho."*

8. The Chazan usually says the words *"Go'al Yisroel"* in a low voice, so that the congregation will not have to interrupt between this and the *Shmoneh Esrei* by answering *Omein.* Some say that the Chazan and the congregation should end *"Go'al Yisroel"* together (audibly) so as to eliminate the problem of *Omein.* Some avoid this problem by beginning *Shmoneh Esrei* before the Chazan recites the *Brocho* of *Go'al Yisroel.*

HILCHOS SHMONEH ESREI

I. TIME

1. The best time to say the *Shmoneh Esrei* is in the morning at *Neitz Hachamah* (sunrise). One can say the *Shmoneh Esrei* until a third of the

"watchers"; that is, to pray together with a minyan, for a congregation united in the proclamation of the Unity and Holiness of G-d is justified in its conviction that its prayers will be answered. *(Sefer Hagaon)*

One should select a G-d-fearing congregation with which to pray. In the synagogue, he should take a permanent place (preferably near the wall) in which to stand for prayer, for then the Almighty will cause His *Shechina* to descend upon that particular place. *(Orach Chayim 90-19)*

R. Yochanan said in connection with this: Whenever the Holy One blessed be He, comes to the synagogue and does not find ten persons there, He instantly becomes angry, for it is said, "Why when I came, was there no man; when I

called no answer?" (Brochos 6b)

"The fact that the synagogue is a miniature sanctuary calls for not only frequent attendance but also proper decorum and respect. R. Chelbo in the name of R. Huna says: "When a man leaves the synagogue he should not take large steps (for he gives the impression that he is running away.)" (Brochos 6-2)

* * * * *

The Biblical city of Chevron was always inhabited by Jews—except for the period 1948-1967 when it was under Jordanian control.

Throughout the years, Jews always wanted to have the *z'chus* (merit) of residing in the city of our forefathers, Avrohom, Yitzchok and Yaakov, and

day has elapsed. However, if one was accidentally unable to say the *Shmoneh Esrei* within a third of the day, he must say the *Shmoneh Esrei* before *Chatzos* (mid-day).

II. THE METHOD OF DAVENING SHMONEH ESREI

1. Before beginning the *Shmoneh Esrei*, one takes three steps back and three steps forward, and then says the words, *"Hashem Sefosai Tiftoch, U'phee Yagid Teheelosecha"* quietly. (By *Mussaf* and *Mincha* one first says the posuk, *"Kee Shem . . ."*)

2. One should say the *Shmoneh Esrei* (and *Kedusha*) with his feet together; but if he does not do so, he still fulfills the *Mitzvah*.

3. The first three *Brochos* and last three *Brochos* of the *Shmoneh Esrei* are each considered one long *Brocho*. Therefore, if one makes an error during any part of the set of three *Brochos*, and finished that *Brocho* and began the next *Brocho*, in the first set he then has to go back to the beginning of the *Shmoneh Esrei*, and in the last set he must return to *Retzai*. If he just erred in the middle of any other *Brocho* and has not as yet gone past the *Brocho*, he corrects himself and continues without going back to the beginning.

4. During the recitation of the *Shmoneh Esrei* we bow four times, at the following places:

a) *"Boruch Atoh Hashem"* (at the beginning of the first paragraph);

to be able to visit and pray at their resting place, the *Meoras Hamachpeilo*. There were times when the Jewish settlement there numbered only a handful of Jews, just enough to make up the required quorum of ten men for the *"minyan,"* and their families.

Many, many years ago, the Jews faced a very serious and depressing situation on *Erev Yom Kippur*. They were faced with the prospect of having to *daven* on the holiest day of the year without a *minyan*. Their "tenth man," the elderly Reb Yitzchok, had suddenly been *"niftar"* (passed away) the day before.

With no means of rapid transportation or communication as we have today, the remainder of the Jewish community could not obtain that desired tenth man before the onset of *Yom Kippur*.

They had no choice but to hope that some Jewish traveler might yet pass through their city and join them. They sent two young men to the outskirts of the city to stand along the roadside looking for the much-hoped-for "tenth man." Another man stood on the high roof of the Chevron Shul, searching in all directions. The only people he could see in the distance were Arab peasants.

The *Shammes* of the Shul prepared ten chairs for ten worshippers, even though he gave up hope of any other Jews coming on *Erev Yom Kippur*. But the Jews of Chevron still waited for some miracle from Heaven.

The man who stood on the roof of

b) *"Boruch Atoh Hashem Mogen Avrohom";*

c) *"Modim";*

d) *"Boruch Atoh Hashem Hatov Shimcha U'L'choh No'eh L'Hodos."*

At the word *"Boruch,"* we bend our knees; at *"Atoh"*, we bow forward; and before saying the word *"Hashem,"* we straighten up.

5. As with all prayers, one should say the *Shmoneh Esrei* with great *kavono* (concentration and devotion). One who did not concentrate, at least during the first *Brocho,* should really be required to daven over again. However, he does not have to repeat *Shmoneh Esrei,* because it is not clear that he will say it with any more concentration than he did the first time.

6. If one's *Tallis* fell partly off while he was saying *Shmoneh Esrei,* he may readjust it. If the *Tallis* fell off completely, he shouldn't pick it up; however, if the situation bothers him, he may do so. The same is true if one dropped his *Siddur* or his glasses.

7. If one stopped while reciting the *Shmoneh Esrei,* for unintentional and unexpected reasons, he does not have to return to the beginning of the *Shmoneh Esrei* unless the time that elapsed was greater than the time necessary for saying the entire *Shmoneh Esrei.* In that case, he would have to repeat the whole *Shmoneh Esrei.*

8. If one talked during the middle of a *Brocho,* he must start again

the Shul kept turning his gaze in the direction of the *Meoras Hamachpeilo* as if imploring the *Avos* to come to their aid. Suddenly he saw a shining pillar of light appear, followed by a shadow. It looked as if a giant door had opened on the side of the *Meoras Hamachpeilo.* The Arabs who were in the vicinity seemed to panic and flee in all directions. The look-out on the roof did not bother staring at them, for his prime concern was finding a Jew.

All of a sudden, there he was. A strange looking man, armed with a staff and dressed in old clothing, was seen coming down the road. A Jew, a tenth man with the most radiant face, was coming to join his fellow Jews so that they could *daven* with a *minyan* on *Yom Kippur.*

It was almost sunset and the time for *Kol Nidre* when the stranger walked into the Shul. It was noticed that the city of Chevron did not seem strange to him. He recognized the Shul and needed no directions. The congregants grouped around him and shook his hand warmly, bidding him *"Shalom."* "Where do you come from?" they asked. The stranger did not reply.

Inside the Shul the stranger was given the seat of honor at the east wall near the *Aron Kodesh.* But the stranger preferred to stand all during the *Tefillos* near a window which looked out upon the *Meoras Hamachpeilo.*

The Jews of Chevron davened with greater inspiration on that *Yom Kippur* than ever before. They were sure that all their *Tefillos,* recited together in one *minyan,* would be more readily

from the beginning of that *Brocho*. However, if he talked in between *Brochos*, he may continue.

9. If one hears the rest of the congregation reciting *Kaddish* or *Kedusha* while he is saying the *Shmoneh Esrei*, he should not respond along with them, but he should just remain silent and listen.

10. One who is intoxicated should not say the *Shmoneh Esrei*.

11. One who is saying the *Shmoneh Esrei* cannot be called to the *Torah*. If one in this situation did go up, he need not start the *Shmoneh Esrei* again from the beginning.

(If one has almost finished the *Shmoneh Esrei*, but has not yet said *"Elokai N'tzor,"* he may go to the *Torah*, if he was called up.)

12. If one arrives for *Mincha* and finds the rest of the congregants already saying the *Shmoneh Esrei*, he should do the same and say *"Ashrei"* later.

13. If one added a *Tefillah* in the *Shmoneh Esrei* unnecessarily (e.g., *Ya'Aleh V'Yovo* or *Zochreinu L'Chayim*), he must return to the beginning of the *Brocho*. If he did not return, he need not repeat the *Shmoneh Esrei*.

14. If one is saying *Shmoneh Esrei* when the *Sh'liach Tzeebur* is up to *Modim* during *Chazoras Ha'Shatz*, he should bow down along with the rest of the congregants, so as to dispel thoughts that he does not wish to

accepted by *Hashem* than if they had davened individually. After all, in unity there is strength.

The time for *Neilah*, the closing service, approached. The blast of the *Shofar* signalled the end of *Yom Kippur*. Friends turned to their neighbors to wish them a Good Year. They turned to the stranger to thank him for enhancing their *Yom Tov*, but he was gone. The two young men who had stood on the road *Erev Yom Kippur* looking for a tenth man, once again went out to look for their guest. All feared that perhaps he had become ill or had died. There was no trace of their mysterious stranger.

The morning after *Yom Kippur*, the *Shammes* awoke from his sleep with a feeling of satisfaction. He had had a

wonderful dream that had helped solve the mystery. The stranger had appeared to him in a dream and revealed that he was our father, Avrohom, who had seen the pain of the Jews of Chevron and, therefore, had come to complete their *minyan*.

Now everything was clear. The stranger had preferred standing by the window gazing at the *Meoras Hamachpeilo* because his soul longed to return to its eternal resting place. The flashes of light that had caused the Arabs to panic had resulted from the opening of the *Meoras Hamachpeilo*.

On the spot where *Avrohom Avinu* stood, the Jews of Chevron built an Ark, and to this day the Shul in Chevron has two Arks.

The two young men who had so

express thankfulness with them. However, this should be done only in the middle of the paragraph and not at the end when he is saying the *Brocho*.

15. If one prays slowly, some authorities hold he should try to say *Kedusha* with the congregants, say the Shmoneh Esrei alone, and bow with them when Modim is said. However, other authorities disagree and believe that saying Shmoneh Esrei with the congregation takes precedence over the recitation of Kedusha.

III. WHAT ONE WHO DID NOT SAY SHMONEH ESREI MUST DO:

1. If one inadvertently forgot to *daven*, he must say the *Shmoneh Esrei* twice during the next *Tefillah* period. For instance, if one did not say the *Shmoneh Esrei* for *Shacharis*, he compensates for the omission by saying *Shmoneh Esrei* twice during *Mincha,* as follows:

He should have in mind that the first *Shmoneh Esrei* is for *Mincha* and the second is the make-up for *Shacharis.* The two prayers should be separated by the recitation of *Ashrei.* However,. *Ashrei* is not said between the two prayers during *Ma'ariv.* In this instance, one need wait only long enough for the time one needs to walk four *Amos.*

2. If, in the above case, one said the two *Shmoneh Esrei* prayers in the reverse order, he must repeat the omitted *Shmoneh Esrei* again. (In the

---

diligently been looking for a tenth man to the *minyan* were blessed in a special way. To one of them, a son was born who was named Avrohom. To the other, a daughter was born and named Soroh. When the children grew up they married and brought added joy and celebration to the Jews of Chevron.

"A person should always get up early to go to Shul to be one of the first ones there, so that even after 100 people come he has the reward of everyone who came after him." (Brochos 47)

* * * * *

Israel had not yet become a state. England's soldiers supervised the Holy Land, and pressured by the Arabs, they made life far from easy for the Jews. Arabs who attacked got away scot-free. Jews who fought back were arrested. Many Jews saw this oppression would continue until they gained complete independence. So they actively fought for their freedom, but the struggle was dangerous. Many Jews ended up in jail as a result.

Prison was certainly not something to look forward to. The life there was rigorous, the food was tasteless, and the endless waiting was terrible. Yet, the prisoners knew that there was one event that could brighten their week. This was the *Shabbos* visit of Rabbi Aryeh Levin.

Rabbi Levin was the unofficial prison chaplain for the Jews. He received no money for it, but he insisted on

above example, if he said the *Shmoneh Esrei* of *Shacharis* before the one for *Mincha*, he must say the *Shmoneh Esrei* of *Shacharis* again.) This third *Shmoneh Esrei* is said conditionally: If reversing the order was a critical defect, this prayer becomes the compensation; if it was not a critical defect, the third *Shmoneh Esrei* is merely an extra prayer offered to Hashem.

3. If one is unsure whether he said the *Shmoneh Esrei,* he says the *Shmoneh Esrei* again as an extra prayer to Hashem. This rule applies to *Shacharis* and *Mincha,* but not to *Ma'ariv* (though, here too, one is *allowed* to repeat the *Shmoneh Esrei*) or to *Mussaf.*

4. One can make restitution for a missed *Shmoneh Esrei* only during the prayer period immediately following. If one does not do so then, he can no longer make restitution.

5. If one did not say the *Shmoneh Esrei* of *Mincha* on *Erev Roch Chodesh,* he says *Shmoneh Esrei* with *Ya'aleh V'Yovoh* twice at *Ma'ariv*—the first time for the *Ma'ariv* and the second for the *Mincha.* If he did not say *"Ya'aleh V'Yovoh"* during either *Shmoneh Esrei,* he need not repeat them.

6. If one compensates for a missed *Ma'ariv Shmoneh Esrei* during *Shacharis,* and he forgot to say *Ya'aleh V'Yovoh* in the second *Shmoneh Esrei,* he need not repeat the prayer. However, he must do so on Chol Ha'moed, if he forgot to say *"Ya'aleh V'Yovoh."*

visiting the prisoners and bringing them cheer. No matter how freezing the weather, no matter how drenching the rain, the prisoners knew that they could count on Rabbi Levin coming to comfort them. He would speak to them, bring them news of their families and the outside world, and boost their morale. Above all, he worked to gain their freedom. At the *Shabbos* prayer services he held in jail, he always recited special *Tefillos* on their behalf. Perhaps, he told the men, his words would find favor in G-d's eyes and would speed their release.

One week, as the jail *minyan* was almost over, a messenger rushed in for Rabbi Levin. He had some important information for the Rabbi. This was most unusual, and everyone knew that something urgent had occurred. So it had. "I'm sorry to tell you, Reb Aryeh, that your daughter has been taken sick. The doctors are with her now, and they ask that you come home immediately." Rabbi Levin did so, obviously concerned. The prisoners were stunned.

The next *Shabbos*, the prisoners were resigned to the fact that because of the continued illness of his daughter, for once they would have to conduct their *minyan* without Rabbi Levin. He would no doubt be busy with personal matters, and too busy to see them.

But Reb Aryeh fooled them. He was there, as usual, and exactly on time.

7. If *Rosh Chodesh* is two days and someone omitted *Ya'aleh V'Yovoh* at *Mincha,* he must, of course, say Shmoneh Esrei twice at *Ma'ariv.* In this case, if he forgot to say *Ya'aleh V'Yovoh* during both the *Ma'ariv* and the make-up *Mincha Shmoneh Esrei* he need not repeat either of the two *Tefillos,* for one does not repeat *Shmoneh Esrei* at night for missing *Ya'aleh V'Yovoh* on *Rosh Chodesh.*

8. If one did not daven the *Mincha Shmoneh Esrei* on *Erev Shabbos,* he says the *Shmoneh Esrei* of *Shabbos* twice at *Ma'ariv.* (Similarly, one who forgets the *Mincha Shmoneh Esrei* on *Shabbos* says the weekday *Shmoneh Esrei* twice at *Ma'ariv,* but in this case, he says "*Atoh Chonantonu*" in the first *Shmoneh Esrei* only. If he forgets to do so in both, he has still fulfilled his obligation.)

IV. LAWS OF MASHIV HORUACH AND MOREED HATAL

1. *Mashiv Horuach* is said beginning with the *Mussaf* prayer of *Shemini Atzeres* until *Mussaf* of the first day of *Pesach* (the *Ashkenazim* still say *Mashiv HoRuach* in the silent *Shmoneh Esrei*), after which some say *Moreed HaTal* instead. (*Ashkenazim* generally do not say *Moreed HaTal.*)

2. If one accidentally said "*Mashiv HoRuach U'Moreed HaGeshem*" during the summer, and remembered this was incorrect before ending the *Brocho,* he must start again from the beginning of the *Brocho.* If he

---

Even his daughter's illness could not keep him away from making his charitable rounds.

The grateful men gathered around him, and he greeted them with his customary radiant smile. Then one of them asked him how his daughter was feeling.

Rabbi Levin's smile faded. "*Boruch Hashem,* she is resting. The doctors say she is doing as well as could be expected. Let us hope for the best." The Rebbe then walked out.

The men were relieved, but one of them still looked glum. "The Rabbi is cheerful for our sake," he told the others, "but the truth is different. I've heard that the Rabbi's daughter is still very sick—paralyzed, in fact. The doctors don't know what to do."

The prisoners felt a deep sadness enshroud them. The Rabbi had done so much for them, and now he was suffering so. Finally, one of them spoke up. "Well, I know what to do. Whenever we're in trouble, the good Rabbi always prays for us. That's the least we can do for him."

The *minyan* began, and Rabbi Levin, distracted as he was, could not help noticing that the prisoners had never before prayed with such fervor, such concentration. Then it came time for the reading of the Torah. The *Kohein* was called up and, after the first portion was read, he asked that a special blessing—a *Mi Shebeirach*—be made. Rabbi Levin listened as the man mentioned the name of Reb Aryeh's daughter, and prayed for the return of her

had already completed the *Brocho,* he must start from the beginning of the *Shmoneh Esrei.*

3. If he realized this error while saying *"Boruch Atoh Hashem,"* he must first complete the *Brocho* by saying *"Lamdeinee Chukechoh"* and then correct his error by returning to the beginning of the *Brocho.* Once he has already said *"Mechayei Hameisim,"* he must return to the beginning of *Shmoneh Esrei,* although he does not have to repeat the sentence of *"Hashem Sefosai Tiftoch."*

4. If one skipped *Mashiv HoRuach* entirely he must repeat the *Shmoneh Esrei.* However, if one accidentally said *Moreed HaTal* instead of *Mashiv HoRuach* during the winter, he does not have to repeat the *Shmoneh Esrei.*

5. If one is uncertain whether he said the proper phrase, he should repeat the *Shmoneh Esrei* only if it is within 30 days (or 90 *Tefillos*) of the time he was to begin saying that sentence. If more than 30 days (or 90 *Tefillos*) have elapsed, it is likely that he uttered the proper phrase and does not repeat the *Shmoneh Esrei.*

V. LAWS OF V'SAIN TAL U'MOTTOR

1. We begin saying *"V'sain Tal U'Mottor"* on the night of December 4 or 5 and continue doing so until *Pesach.* In *Eretz Yisroel, "V'Sain Tal*

---

health. Then the man went on, "And I want to add a personal donation. I wish to give up a day of my life on her behalf."

Rabbi Levin was taken aback, but the idea caught on. The next man called up added his prayers, and said that he wanted to donate a week of his life. The third man gave up two weeks, the next a month, and so on.

Rabbi Levin watched all this in disbelief. At the conclusion, he went over to each and every man, and thanked him for what he had done. "What have I ever done to deserve such generosity on your part?" he asked in gratitude.

When Rabbi Levin arrived home, he was met by the doctor, who was smiling broadly. "I have good news, Reb Aryeh. Just a little while ago, your daughter's temperature suddenly started going down. She even began regaining some feeling in her hands. I think she's on her way to recovery. I have no idea what caused it."

Rabbi Levin smiled to himself. "Well," he said, "I think I do."

R. Yehoshua ben Levi said to his son, "Wake up early to go to Shul in order to live a long life."

(Brochos 8)

It is a positive commandment to say *Krias Shema* in the morning and evening as it says (*Devorim* 6) "And you should speak in them when you lie down and get up" which means at the time of sleeping and the time of getting up.

G-d wants His nation to accept upon themselves His kingdom and to proclaim His unity day and night all the days of their lives. By saying *Krias*

U'Mottor" is recited beginning on the 7th of *Cheshvan*. If an American comes to *Eretz Yisroel* for a brief visit during the winter, and does not intend to stay, he does not say *"V'sain Tal U'Mottor"* while in Israel before December 5th, the day it would be required in the U.S.

2. If one said *"V'Sain Tal U'Mottor"* during the summer by accident, he must repeat the *Shmoneh Esrei* correctly. If it is a country that requires rain in the summertime like the United States, he repeats the *Shmoneh Esrei* with a *T'nai*. If he did this between the 7th of Cheshvan and the night of December 4th and 5th, it is questionable whether he should repeat the *Shmoneh Esrei,* so he should do so with a *T'nai* (in a conditional manner, as discussed in Section III, #2).

3. If one forgot to say *"V'Sain Tal U'Mottor"* during the winter, and remembered before finishing the *Brocho* of *"Mevoreich Ha'Shonim,"* he can insert the words there and continue with the rest of the prayer. If he remembered the error before *"Sh'ma Koleinu,"* he should insert *"V'Sain Tal U'Mottor"* in the *Sh'ma Koleinu,* before *"Kee Atoh Shomea Tefillah."*

If, however, he had already said the words, *"Boruch Atoh Hashem"* before *"Shomeia Tefillah,"* he should finish the *Brocho* with the words *"Lamdeinee Chukecha"* instead. He should then say *"V'Sain Tal U'Mottor,"* and proceed with *"Kee Atoh Shomeia."* If he realized the

---

Shema one reinforces the feeling that G-d is watching him.

When reciting the *Shema*, it is customary to place the right hand over one's eyes and to slightly prolong the word *"Echad."* This is done in order to concentrate while affirming the unity of *Hashem* and our acceptance of His dominion over the entire universe. Throughout the centuries, Jews have offered up their lives for their faith, often proclaiming with their very last breath, *"Shema Yisroel."* (Brochos 19b)

He who reads the *Krias Shema* when he ends the first *posuk* should say quietly, *"Boruch Shem K'vod Malchuso Le'Olom Vo'ed."* Then he says *V'Ahavto* "You should love G-d your G-d," until the end. Why is *"Boruch*

Shem" said? When Yaakov gathered his sons in Egypt by his death bed he commanded them and inspired them that they should follow the path of G-d as their forefathers, Avrohom, Yitzchok and Yaakov had done. He also taught them how to know G-d. He asked, "Is there anyone here who does not accept completely the faith of G-d?" They answered, "Hear *Yisroel* G-d is our G-d and G-d is one." Then Yaakov answered, *"Boruch Shem K'Vod Malchuso Le'Olom Vo'ed."* Therefore, it is customary that *Klal Yisroel* says this praise which Yaakov said after *Shema Yisroel.* (Pesachim 56, Rambam 8:1, Hilchos Krias Shema)

Rabbi Yisroel Salanter, the great master of *Mussar* (Ethics), pointed

omission before *"Yeeh'yu L'Rotzon,"* he must return to *"Boreich Oleinu"* and continue the prayer from there. If he has already taken one step back at the conclusion of the *Shmoneh Esrei,* though, he must repeat the entire *Shmoneh Esrei.*

VI. LAWS OF THE SHMONEH ESREI DURING ASERES YEMEI TESHUVA

1. During the *Aseres Yemei Teshuva* (from *Rosh Hashono* through *Yom Kippur),* if one forgets *"Zochreinu Lechayim," "Mi Komocho," "Uksov Lechayim"* or *"B'sefer Chaim,"* he should continue the *Shmoneh Esrei* and not go back at all if he had already completed the *Brocho;* he is *Yotzai* the *Shmoneh Esrei* without them.

2. During these days one who says *"Ha'Kail Ha'Kodosh"* instead of *"Ha'Melech Ha'Kodosh"* was not *Yotzai* and must repeat *Shmoneh Esrei* from the beginning. However, one who says *"Melech Ohaiv Tzedaka U'Mishpot"* instead of *"Hamelech Hamishpot"* need not repeat *Shmoneh Esrei* since he stated the word *Melech.*

VII. COMPLETING THE SHMONEH ESREI

1. After completing the *Shmoneh Esrei,* one takes three steps backwards, beginning with the left foot.

2. After one has taken the three steps back, he should remain there for

---

out that it is insufficient for the individual to concentrate on these aspects of *Hashem's* dominion alone. He must be careful to also accept the absolute dominion of *Hashem* upon himself, in a very personal way. Only then will he have fulfilled this commandment properly.

"The Kohein annointed for war, said to the army, "Hear Yisroel." Why this posuk? G-d said to the Jews, "If you say Krias Shema of morning and evening you won't fall into the enemies hands." (Sotah 42)

"Krias Shema shouldn't be lenient in your eyes" because the 248 words including the words "Baruch Shem K'vod Malchuso L'Olom Vo'ed" are like the 248 limbs in your body. G-d said, "If you say

Krias Shema in the right time, I will watch over you." (Medrash Tanchuma)

The Torah relates that when Yaakov met his long-lost son, Yosef, in *Mitzrayim,* the latter fell upon his father's neck and wept. There is no mention, however, of a similar response from Yaakov. Surely he, too, must have been overcome by great emotion upon meeting his beloved son for whom he had grieved twenty-two years. *Rashi* explains that Yaakov did not weep or show any emotion whatsoever because he was reciting the *Shema.* The *Malbim* observes that Yaakov chose this particular moment to recite the *Shema* in order to show that his love for his Creator was still greater than his immense love for his long-lost son, Yosef. This legacy of

at least the time necessary to walk four *amos*. When davening with a *Minyan* it is best to wait until the Chazan starts *Kedusha* or at least until *Chazoras Ha'Shatz*.

3. If one person saying *Shmoneh Esrei* is standing directly in front of a second, the first should not take the three steps backwards if there is not enough room to do so, (e.g., if he will enter within four *Amos* of the one in back.) Rather, he should wait until the second one has finished the *Shmoneh Esrei*, and then take the three steps. One is not allowed to walk in front of someone saying *Shmoneh Esrei*, or sit within four *amos* of him.

4. After finishing the *Shmoneh Esrei*, one should try not to speak until after he has said *Tachanun*.

VIII. CHAZORAS HA'SHATZ (THE CHAZAN'S REPETITION OF THE SHMONEH ESREI)

1. The *Sh'liach Tzeebur* should say the *Shmoneh Esrei* quietly to himself with the rest of the congregation. Then he should repeat the *Shmoneh Esrei* aloud, to fulfill the *Mitzvah* of *Chazoras Ha'Shatz*.

2. When beginning the *Chazoras Ha'Shatz*, the Chazan should take the usual three steps backward and three steps forward and say, "*Hashem Sefosai Tiftoch*." However, at the end of the *Chazoras*

---

intense love for *Hakadosh Baruch Hu* is what our Patriarch, Yaakov, bequeathed to his children as a heritage for all generations.

"*Jerusalem was destroyed because they did not say the* Krias Shema *of morning and night.*" (Shabbos 119b)

"*When a child starts to speak, his father should teach him Torah and* Krias Shema. *Which part of* Krias Shema? *The first posuk.*" (Succah 42)

Rabbi Akiva said: In Shema *we say,* "With all your Soul," *implying that you should love and obey* Hashem *even if it takes your life.* Shimon ben Azzai said, "With all your Soul"—with your soul's lifeblood, till your dying breath. (Brochos 61b)

"*With all your Soul*"—*with every part of your soul, man has to praise* Hashem *with every breath he draws.* (Tehillim 105:6)

LOVE OF HASHEM

"All my plans are ruined by this one crack!"

Ever since the king had heard of the discovery of a huge diamond in the royal mines he had dreamed of making this precious stone the centerpiece of his crown. But when it arrived at his palace he noticed that a large crack on one side of the diamond marred its perfect beauty.

"There is only one thing His Majesty can do," advised the royal jeweler. "He must order the stone to be cut into smaller gems and each of them will be a perfect diamond."

Ha'Shatz, he does not take three steps backward until the end of the full *Kaddish* when he steps back for *"Oseh Sholom."* The three steps backward for *"Oseh Sholom"* are reckoned as the necessary steps for the *Chazoras Ha'Shatz;* thus if the *Sh'liach Tzeebur* must leave the *Omud* before the full *Kaddish* is said, he should take the three steps back first. (e.g. In case of *Tachanun* or *Krias Hatorah,* he takes the three steps back before he moves out of his place.)

3. One who does not know how to daven properly may daven along with the *Sh'liach Tzeebur,* word-for-word, to fulfill the *Mitzvah,* but he should not answer *"Boruch Hu U'Voruch Shemo"* and *Omein.* One who is late should also do the same.

4. The *Sh'liach Tzeebur* can begin *Chazoras Ha'Shatz* immediately after the *Tzeebur* has completed the *Shmoneh Esrei* and he need not wait for latecomers to finish. There should, however, be a total of ten men who have finished, including the *Shliach Tzeebur.*

5. Some have the custom to stand throughout *Chazoras Ha'Shatz.*

6. One must answer *"Boruch Hu U'Voruch Shemo"* and *"Omein"* to every *Brocho.* One should be careful to enunciate the word *Omein* correctly; namely to make sure not to swallow the *'nun'* or to change the vowel sound of the *'aleph.'* Some make the mistake of answering *Omein* before the *Brocho* has been completed, or to extend the *Omein* longer than necessary, or to answer the *Omein* late. These practices are incorrect.

"But if I do that," protested the worried king, "I won't have the large stone I want for my crown. No, I must find another solution."

The finest craftsmen from near and far were summoned to the palace but gave the same suggestion. "The diamond must be cut!"

Just as the king was about to resign himself to this verdict, he was pleasantly surprised to hear one jeweler announce:

"Your Highness, if you will please permit me to work on this diamond, I believe I can make it ready by tomorrow for use as a large and brilliant centerpiece for the royal crown."

Permission was granted. As the jeweler worked behind the closed doors of the palace workshop, the king paced nervously outside. The jeweler worked for a day and a night without a pause. The sound of his polishing and scraping filled the palace with a sense of wonder and mystery.

Then came the great moment! The king was invited to come and see the finished product.

On the table before him he saw the great diamond polished to a perfect smoothness except for the side with the crack. There the jeweler had etched the royal coat of arms, a beautiful rose in which the crack itself perfectly served as the stem.

The grateful king commissioned the

7. One is permitted to answer *Omein* to a *Brocho* even though he did not hear the end of the *Brocho*, as long as he knows which *Brocho* has just been said.

8. There should not be any talking while *Chazoras Ha'Shatz* is being said. One who must leave the Shul should try to remain there at least through *Kedusha*.

9. One should stand with his feet together while *Kedusha* is said, and should elevate himself slightly three times at the words, *"Kodosh, Kodosh, Kodosh,"* and once each by the *"Boruch K'vod,"* and *"Yimloch Hashem."*

10. If the *Sh'liach Tzeebur* is unable to continue, anyone else who is asked to proceed should do so without hesitating. He should commence at the beginning of the last *Brocho* started by his predecessor. However, if the *Sh'liach Tzeebur* had been in the middle of the first three or last three *Brochos* of the *Shmoneh Esrei,* the replacement should return to the beginning of the appropriate section.

11. If the *Sh'liach Tzeebur* forgot to add the special prayers for *Shabbos* or *Yom Tov,* and he realizes his error before he finishes the *Shmoneh Esrei,* he should return to the beginning of the appropriate section (i.e. *Yismach Moshe* on *Shacharis* of *Shabbos* and to *Atoh B'chartonu* on *Yom Tov).*

clever jeweler to place the stone in the coronation crown and then rewarded him handsomely for converting a flaw into a masterpiece.

The Maggid of Dubnow explains the Talmid's interpretation of the commandment to "love G-d with all your heart," contained in the *Shema* prayer, as referring to both hearts—both the good and evil inclinations. Serving Hashem with the good inclination—the *Yetzer Tov*—is a rather simple matter. But how does one serve Him with the evil inclination—the *Yetzer Horo*—which urges him to sin?

The *Yetzer Horo* is the flaw in our otherwise perfect, gem-like souls. But we have the ability to transform this flaw into a masterpiece. Each evil trait can be utilized for good. Envy can be used to spur one on to greater ac-

complishment in Torah study. Energy available for destruction can be changed into power for constructive efforts.

If our love for *Hashem* is complete we can serve Him with even the bad in us. For only if we serve with "both our hearts" do we show a whole-hearted love for the King of Kings.

*　*　*　*　*

WITH ALL YOUR HEART

In the early decades of this century, a son of the Chofetz Chaim named Avraham, passed away. He had been a brilliant, outstanding Talmud scholar, and while still a young man, had produced many *"chiddushim"*—original explanations and clarifications in the Talmud.

It was a sad, mournful day when the

12. When the *Sh'liach Tzeebur* says *Modim*, the rest of the congregants should bow and say the *Modim D'Rabbonon*.

13. *Birchos Kohanim* is added during *Shacharis*, during *Mincha* on a *Ta'anis*, and throughout *Yom Kippur*, for this is when the *Kohanim* used to *duchan*. It can be said only with a *Minyan* present.

IX. DUCHANING—The Blessing of the Kohanim

1. The *Kohanim duchan* every day in certain parts of *Eretz Yisroel*. In America there are different customs. *Ashkenazim duchan* only on *Yom Tov* while *Sephardim* do the same as in *Eretz Yisroel*.

2. Before *Birchos Kohanim*, a *Levi* washes the *Kohein's* hands. If no *Levi* is available for this task, a *B'chor* (first-born) should do so. If no *B'chor* is available, the *Kohein* should wash his own hands rather than let a *Yisroel* do so.

3. The *Kohanim* should *duchan* in their stockings—they cannot do so while wearing shoes or while barefoot.

4. The *Kohanim* should go up towards the *Aron Hakodesh* before the end of *"R'tzai"* in the *Shmoneh Esrei*.

5. Outside *Eretz Yisroel* the Chazan then calls out, '*Kohanim*' and the congregation replies: '*Am Kedoshechah Ko'omure'*.

6. The congregation should not look at the *Kohanim's* fingers while the blessing is being said, therefore the *Kohanim* put their fingers inside the *Tallis*.

funeral procession followed the coffin slowly through the town of Radun out to the Jewish cemetery. There the Chofetz Chaim began his *hesped*—his words of praise and lament for the son he had lost. He said (in part):

"In the terrible years of persecution and pillage, 1648-49, the Almighty saw fit to pour out His wrath on dozens of holy Jewish communities in Eastern Europe. Thousands of Jews were slain and slaughtered in holy martyrdom. In one small village a widow lived with her only son, a lad more precious to her than anything in the world. Her little house stood at the edge of the village, and when the accursed hordes of Chmielnitzki came on their rampage, they fell on that little house at once,

and slew the widow's only son right before her eyes."

"Too thunderstruck to say a word, the woman stood there mute in her grief, her hands held out, palms facing upward to heaven. Her eyes were dry; the wound was too deep for tears. But she whispered something to the Creator, standing thus before Him:

" 'Divine Sovereign of the world, in every human being you did implant a heart, to enable him to love You; I have always tried to have love for You. Every day, morning and evening, I said the *Shema*—"And you shall love the L-rd, your G-d, with all your heart and with all your soul, and with all your might." Only, sinful servant of Yours that I am, I could not really love You

7. The *Kohanim* should not return to their seats until after the *Kaddish* has been said.

8. It is preferable that the *Sh'liach Tzeebur* not be a *Kohein*. If the *Sh'liach Tzeebur* is a *Kohein* and there are other *Kohanim* present, he should not *duchan*. However, if he is the only *Kohein* there, someone else should announce the *Birchas Kohanim* word by word as the *Sh'liach Tzeebur* does and he should face the congregation and *duchan*. Immediately afterwards he should turn back to the *Omud* and complete the *Tefillah*.

9. If a *Kohein* has a blemish on his hands, face, or feet, and feels that people will stare at him if he goes to *duchan,* he should not do so and he should leave the Shul before *Birchos Kohanim*. If, however, the blemish is in a covered area, he should *duchan*. A *Rav* should be consulted.

10. It is best not to ask a *Mechallel Shabbos* (one who desecrates the Shabbos) to *duchan* even if no other *Kohein* is in the Shul.

11. A *Kohein* who is married to a divorced woman may not *duchan* or be called to the Torah as a *Kohein*. If he is called to the Torah, he should be called as a *Yisroel.* The children from such a marriage are not considered *Kohanim*.

---

with all my heart, because half of it was filled with love for my boy, whom I bore. Now, however, Your will has been done, and my son has been taken away from me. Now I can love You with *all* my heart.'

"All my life," the Chofetz Chaim continued, "I wished to love the L-rd with all my heart. Yet, I am only a creature of flesh and blood, and I am the father of sons. It is only human nature for a father to have compassion and love for his children. Willingly or not, I divided my heart into segments, giving a part to each of my children. Now that the Almighty has seen fit to take one of them from me, I am left with another section of my heart with which to love Him. . . ."

* * * * *

Once, in the days of Rabbi Tanchum, there was a drought. People

came to him and pleaded: "Rabbi, decree a general fasting." He decreed it for one day, then extended it to a second and a third day, but still no rain fell.

He went and addressed the people: "My sons, fill your heart with compassion towards one another, and the Almighty will have compassion on you."

While the people were distributing alms among the poor, they saw a man talking to his ex-wife and giving her money. The Rabbi sent for them, and when they came, he asked the man: "What is she to you?" The man answered, "She is my ex-wife."

"And why did you give her money?"

The man replied: "I saw she had fallen on evil days and I had compassion on her."

Whereupon Rabbi Tanchum immediately raised his face upwards and prayed: "L-rd of the Universe! If he

X. LAWS OF TACHANUN

1. *Tachanun* is said after *Shmoneh Esrei* during *Shacharis* and *Mincha*, except on the following occasions: *Shabbos, Yom Tov, Rosh Chodesh, Chol Hamoed, Erev Rosh Hashono, Erev Yom Kippur, Chanukah, Lag Ba'omer*, and *Tu B'shvat*, the days between *Yom Kippur* and *Succos* (some don't say it till *Roch Chodesh Cheshvan*), *Purim* and *Shushan Purim* of *Adar Rishon* and *Adar Shainee*, the 15th of *Shevat*, the entire month of *Nissan, Pesach Shainee*, the days between *Rosh Chodesh Sivan* and *Shavuos* (some don't say it till the 12th of *Sivan*), the 9th of *Av*, the 15th of *Av*, and the *Mincha* before all the above days except the *Mincha* before *Erev Rosh Hashono* or *Erev Yom Kippur*, when a *Chosson* (groom) is present, when an *ovel* (mourner) is present during the seven days of his mourning, or when a *Bris* is performed in the Shul. If the *Bris* is performed elsewhere, the congregation where the father of the child, the *mohel*, or the *sandek* (godfather) davens does not say *Tachanun* at *Shacharis*. At *Mincha* these three do not say *Tachanun*, but the rest of the congregation do.

2. During days when *Selichos* is said, if a *chosson*, a father of a newborn son, a *mohel*, or a *sandek* is present, we do not say *Tachanun* but we do say partial *Selichos*.

3. While saying *Tachanun*, one "falls on his face," meaning that one

who is not obliged to support her was filled with compassion when he saw her in need, then how much more should You have compassion on us, your children who depend entirely on your help."

At that very moment the rain began to fall.

* * * * *

A youth fought many battles for his country. He distinguished himself, and in return received the highest decoration. Then he became involved in a plot and was thrown into prison. When his case was about to be tried, he put on his decoration, which was conferred only very rarely. When his accuser saw this decoration, he rose and said: "I withdraw my charge against this man, for a man who has

saved his country from great distress and danger is incapable of wishing to destroy it."

Still, the man was accused a second time. He brought his children along to court. When the judge saw these innocent and tender little ones whom, in obedience to the letter of the law, he ought to deprive of their father, he felt so moved that he pardoned him.

A third time the man was summoned to defend himself. This time, while the proceedings were still in progress, he tore off his coat and shirt and silently pointed at the horrible scars that remained from the severe wounds he had suffered in battle. Again he was forgiven.

Our own experiences in life can be compared to his. We pray to G-d: "Forgive us since Thy great and holy

rests his face on his arm as a sign of repentance. A person who is right-handed uses his left hand for this. When one is wearing *Tefillin*, though, he should use the hand without the *Tefillin*.

4. One "falls on his face" during *Tachanun* only if a *Sefer Torah* is present.

5. After *Tachanun*, the prayers of *Chatzee Kaddish, Ashrei, Lamnatzeiach,* and *Uvo L'Tzion* are said. On Mondays, Thursdays, and special days, the Torah is read before *Ashrei.*

6. For those who daven *Nusach Sephard,* the *Tefillah* of *Shacharis* concludes with the *Shir Shel Yom, Ein K'Elokeinu* and *Oleinu,* followed by *Kaddish.* Those who daven *Nusach Ashkenaz* conclude with *Oleinu* and *Shir Shel Yom.* They do not recite *Ein K'Elokeinu* except on *Shabbos* and *Yom Tov.*

XI. HILCHOS KRIAS HATORAH

1. The Torah is read on *Shabbos* morning, *Shabbos* afternoon, Monday and Thursday mornings, Jewish holidays (only in the morning) and fast days (both morning and afternoon). On *Shabbos* morning, after *Shacharis,* an entire *Sedra* (and sometimes two) is read; while on *Shabbos* afternoon, as well as on Monday and Thursday mornings, only the first segment of the next week's *Sedra* (usually until *Sheini*) is read.

2. If a congregation was unable to read the Torah on a particular

Name has been called over us. After all, we are Jews, sons of the people who stood at Sinai, which Thou hast chosen from all peoples on earth. Thy Name is forever linked with ours, hence forgive us for the sake of Thy Name which has been called over us. Did we not bear Thy Law throughout the ages in a spirit of self-sacrifice? Did we not suffer greatly for Thy Torah more than any other people on earth? Forgive us for the sake of those who sacrificed their lives."

* * * * *

It was prayer that saved the Jews of Yerushalayim at the time of Napoleon. Reb Mordechai was praying at the *Kosel HaMa'aravi,* the Western Wall, when suddenly five brilliantly white letters *"aleph"* appeared. He stared at them for a while, and then they seemed to vanish. Reb Mordechai was frightened, not knowing what they meant.

The next day, his fears seemed to be confirmed. He learned that the Pasha (the Turkish ruler of Yerushalayim) had decided that all Jews living within ten blocks of the *Kosel* had to vacate their homes immediately. Not waiting for the Jews to comply, the Pasha's soldiers began looting the Jews' homes. Now Reb Mordechai knew what the five "alephs" represented: the words *"Omar Oyeiv Erdof Asig Achalek Sholol*—the enemy said, 'I will pursue, I will overtake, I will divide the spoils.' "

All seemed lost. Many despaired

Shabbos morning, the entire Sedra should be read on Shabbos afternoon. If the Torah reading was missed one week, that Sedra should be read first on the next Shabbos, followed by the appropriate Sedra. If a double Sedra (such as Tazriah-Metzorah) was missed, both Sedras should be read the next week, followed by that week's Sedra. (It is questionable whether one can compensate for a missed Sedra if the current Sedra is from a different Sefer of Chumash as in the case of missing Bechukosai, which is followed by Bamidbar).

3. An Aliya to the Torah refers to calling up an individual to the Bimah to say Borchu, Boruch Hashem and make the Brochos ("Asher Bochar Bonu" and "Asher Nossan Lonu") over the Torah. There are three Aliyos on Shabbos afternoon, Monday and Thursday mornings, Purim, Chanukah, and fast days. There are four Aliyos on Rosh Chodesh and Chol Hamoed of Pesach and Succos. There are five Aliyos on Pesach, Shavuos, Succos and Rosh Hashono, and six Aliyos on Yom Kippur morning, followed by Maftir and the Haftorah. On Shabbos morning, there are seven Aliyos, followed by Maftir and the Haftorah. The person called for the first Aliya should be a Kohein; the second, a Levi; and the remaining Aliyos (except for those after the seventh Aliya) should go to Yisraelim.

4. The first Aliya is reserved for a Kohein even if he is an am ha'oretz

but not Reb Mordechai. He prayed to heaven and his prayers gave him added incentive to persevere. He urged his fellow Jews not to give up hope.

That very day the unexpected happened. Reb Mordechai received instructions to present himself immediately to the Pasha. When he arrived, the Pasha said, "I have just received word that the army of Napoleon is approaching. I am desperate. If Napoleon comes, all is lost. My only hope rests with you. You must pray to your G-d not to let Napoleon take over the city."

Reb Mordechai looked at the Pasha angrily and replied, "How can you expect the Jews to pray for you if you ordered us to stay away from the holy Kosel?"

Upon hearing this, the Pasha immediately reversed his evil decree. The Jews, once again allowed to live and pray at the Kosel, prayed for the safety of Yerushalayim. The city was saved as the result of prayer.

"G-d said to the Jews, Be careful with prayer since it is greater than sacrifices. Even if a person is not worthy to be answered, even with all the kindness he did in this world, if he prays sincerely, G-d will do kindness for him" (Medrash Tanchuma)

Sometimes, Hashem's assistance is given directly to individuals.

One such case happened during the dark days of World War I. A conquering colonel decided to show off his power by ordering a Rav to bathe with women. The Rav, well aware of the halochos against this, refused, and the

54

(ignorant person) and there is a *talmid chochom* (scholar) present. If no *Kohein* is present, a *talmid chochom* who is a *Yisroel* takes precedence over a *Levi* who is an *am ha'oretz*. If a *Kohein* is present but cannot be called to the Torah (such as when he is not fasting on a *Ta'anis*), the *Kohein* should leave the Shul, while the *Levi* or *Yisroel* is called up.

5. If a *Yisroel* had been called for the first *Aliya*, and then a *Kohein* enters, the *Kohein* can take his place unless the *Yisroel* had already said the name of Hashem in the first *Brocho*. If the *Kohein* is called up, the *Yisroel* who was replaced should wait by the *Bimah* and should be given the third *Aliya*, to confirm to the congregation that he is indeed fit for an *Aliya*.

6. If no *Levi* is present, the *Kohein* is given the second *Aliya* as well. If no *Kohein* is available, and a *Levi* is called for the first *Aliya* instead, another *Levi* should not be called up for the second *Aliya*, because this might imply that the first *Levi* is unfit, or that he is a *Kohein* (The second *Aliya* cannot be given to a *Kohein*.)

7. The third *Aliya* on *Shabbosim* and *Yomim Tovim* should preferably be given to a *talmid chochom*. An atheist should not be called to the Torah at any time. A father and son or two brothers should not have consecutive *Aliyos*.

8. At least ten *pesukim* must be read during *Krias HaTorah*, unless

colonel vowed to kill him. When the townsfolk heard this, they pleaded with the Rav to flee for his life. However, the Rav replied that he had full faith and would pray to *Hashem* who had saved the Jews of Egypt at their time of need, and who, he prayed, would save him as well. Just as the Rav was engaged in fervent prayer, the colonel rode through the town and, furious at seeing the Rav, came charging towards him. Just as he was about to make a lunge at the Rav with his sword, the colonel's horse stumbled to the ground. The colonel was thrown high into the air and landed on his sword, dying instantly. The Rav knew that this miracle had been engineered by none other than *Hashem*, and his thanks to the Almighty never ceased until the end of his life.

RAIN OR DEATH

The following is a story related by a Yemenite Jew about his grandfather and himself.

"Mother, may I have another piece of bread?" I asked. "I'm so hungry."

"I know you are," mother said as she patted my cheek. "But if you eat any more today, you won't have enough for tomorrow. I know it's hard for you, but everyone is hungry. You must be brave."

You see, there was famine at that time in the land of *Taymon* (Yemen). Famine means no food, and no food meant hunger. All this happened seventy years ago. Yet, I remember it clearly even today. For over a year, no rain had fallen and I remember how the wheat and corn shriveled and dried up in the fields.

the shorter reading constitutes a complete topic in itself, which is only true of *Parshas Amoleik*. At least three *pesukim* must be read for each *Aliya,* and the *Baal Korei* should not stop less than three *pesukim* from the end of a *parsha.*

9. When one is called for an *Aliya,* he should go to the *Bimah,* in the shortest way possible, to show his desire to reach the Torah quickly. If both ways are equally short, he should ascend on the right side. After completing the *Aliya,* he should return to his seat via the longer path.

10. When making the *Brochos* on the Torah, one should hold both handles of the Torah. (This does not apply to the *Sephardim* who have no handles on their *Sifrei Torah.*) The *Ashkenazic* custom is for the one called up to hold one handle with the right hand during the *Kriah* and the *Baal Korei* to hold the other. One should also be shown the place to be read before making the *Brochos.* If he is shown the correct general area but not the exact place, he need not repeat the *Brocho.* However, if the general area shown him is also incorrect, he must repeat the *Brocho.* After being shown the place, one should touch the place, preferably with his prayer shawl, or any part of the *Sefer,* according to his custom, and then kiss this with his *Tzitzis* or a *gartel;* however, one should not actually kiss the parchment itself.

11. If one mistakenly said the *Brocho* of *"Asher Nossan Lonu"* instead

Tu B'Shvat was different that year. Not only was there no new fruit upon which to recite the *"Shehechiyanu"* but no fruit at all grew upon the trees. Market places were empty of their usually busy fruit stands.

For over a year, there was almost no rain. Without rain nothing could grow. Whatever food could be bought was very expensive, and the Jews of Taymon were poor.

What do you do to bring rain? You pray. And so every afternoon we all went to Shul, men, women and children. From there we marched through the streets. Every man wore a *tallis* and *tefillin.* At the head of the procession the Rabbi and a few others carried *Sifrei Torah.* We said *Tehillim* and many cried aloud mournfully. We knew that if rain didn't fall soon, we

would all starve to death.

As we were proceeding through the streets, we met the Arab procession. The Moslem Arabs also marched through the streets every afternoon, praying in their own fashion, and every day we passed each other. Suddenly, one day all praying stopped, and both groups, Moslems and Jews, stood still. An Arab had climbed on a high, flat rock, and began shouting. We all turned to listen as he shouted with all his might.

"Listen, my friends. Do you want to know who is responsible for our hunger? The Jews—no one else. I tell you, they can bring rain whenever they wish to. There is a story which they tell about the time when they sorely needed rain in Palestine, just as we do now. One of their learned, pious men made

of *"Asher Bochar Bonu,"* but had not yet completed the *Brocho,* he should go back and say the *Brocho* of *"Asher Bochar Bonu"* before the Torah is read. However, if he had already completed the *Brocho,* he should say *"Asher Bochar Bonu"* after the *Aliya* is completed.

12. The person called up for an *Aliya* must say the *Brochos* loudly enough for a *Minyan* to hear and respond. He must not join the *Baal Korei* in reading the Torah aloud, for only one voice reading the Torah can be heard. However, he must read it quietly to himself. This does not apply when one is in the middle of *Birchas Krias Shema,* in which case he just makes the *Brochos* but keeps quiet during the *Kriah.*

13. There must be three people on the *Bimah* during the *Krias HaTorah.* This is true even if the *Baal Korei* gets an *Aliya.*

14. Even if two *Sifrei Torah* are used at one time, no person should receive more than one *Aliya.*

15. Two boys who become *Bar Mitzvah* on the same *Shabbos* should not read the Torah or the *Haftorah* together.

16. The *Sefer Torah* should be covered between one *Aliya* and another.

17. If the *Baal Korei* errs in pronouncing a word, and the error results in an incorrect interpretation of the word, he must go back and repeat the word correctly.

18. If a mistake is found in the *Sefer Torah,* another Torah must be used. A *Rav* should be consulted on this matter.

a circle in the sand with a stick, within which he stood, and he said, 'Almighty Master, I will not leave this circle until You send us rain.' That's all he did, and soon rain fell. Ask the Jews if what I say is true. Go ahead, ask them. They know the story about *Choni HaMa'agol,* Choni the circlemaker."

"I tell you, my friends," the Arab continued hysterically, "the power to bring rain is given to the Jews. In every generation, there is at least one Jew who can cause rain whenever he wants to. Only these Jews don't want to. They would rather starve, as long as we starve too. Do you think it is natural that no rain has fallen for a whole year? I tell you, this is their doing. Let's

go to the king and have him issue a decree saying that either the Jews bring rain or they die."

I couldn't see any truth in his accusations but the Arabs drank in every word. They were eager to find a scapegoat—someone or something to blame for their misfortunes. We saw three Moslems set out for the palace, which was but ten minutes away, since this was the capital city of Taymon.

Less than an hour later, the three Moslems were back, waving a piece of paper excitedly. They handed it to their friend on the rock, and he read it in triumph: "Be it known that the Jews of Taymon must bring rain in the next three days. If they fail, they are all to be

19. When another *Sefer Torah* has to be taken out, seven *Aliyos* should be given from that second Torah if it can be done without much difficulty. The portion already read need not be repeated. If a mistake was found during the reading of *Maftir,* a different *Sefer Torah* need not be taken out, but it should be completed. (However, if the mistake in *Maftir* was found on a *Yom Tov* or a *Shabbos* or *Arba Parshios,* when the *Maftir* is not the repetition of a portion already read, a *Rav* should be consulted.)

20. If a mistake was found in the Torah and no other Torah is available, a *Rav* should be consulted. A final *Brocho* is said at the end of the *laining* (reading). In the case where two letters touch, the *Aliyos* continue with *Brochos* but no *Maftir* is *lained.* However, in regard to *Brochos,* a *Rav* should be consulted.

21. If the *Sefer Torah* is torn between one *kelaf* (piece of parchment) and another, it is definitely *kosher,* provided more than half of the parchments are still stitched together.

22. If the ink was properly black when the *Sefer Torah* was written, but it has changed color slowly as the Torah aged, the Torah remains

killed." The Arabs talked excitedly among themselves. The Jews returned home with a feeling of fear and despair.

That night I couldn't sleep. As I tossed and turned, I heard my grandfather chanting prayers softly. My saintly grandfather with his long, white beard, continued to sob and to pray all through the night.

We spent the next three days in Shul, fasting and praying. Prayers were even more fervent than on *Yom Kippur.* By the third day, everything was the same, until Grandfather went up to the Rabbi late in the afternoon, and asked permission to lead the *Mincha* prayers. That was strange, for Grandfather had never led any service before. Even more strange were his eyes. They seemed to shine, and I thought they were seeing far beyond our vision. When he prayed there wasn't a dry eye in the Shul.

When the davening was over,

Grandfather did a second strange thing. He asked everyone to go outside. We all gathered in the street; then he came out. He seemed an angel from heaven. The people drew back before him. In his hand was a stick. I half-guessed what was about to occur.

Standing in the sand of the street, Grandfather carefully drew a circle around himself with the stick. To my dying day I shall always remember his words as he turned his eyes heavenward:

"Master of the Universe, do you want Your children to die? All our lives we try to obey Your commands, no matter how hard they are. We don't cheat; we don't steal. The scales we use to measure the things we sell are correct. It is hard for us to earn a living, but we struggle, for it is Your will. We beg You, have mercy on us. It is so easy for You to send rain."

Grandfather paused, and the silence

kosher. However, if the ink changed color shortly after the Torah was written, the Torah is *possul* (not valid), for this indicates that the original ink was defective. A *Mechallel Shabbos* (desecrator of the *Shabbos*) cannot write a *Sefer Torah* or blacken in the letters.

23. One should not stand with his back to the *Sefer Torah*. Whoever sees a *Sefer Torah* fall to the floor should fast or give money to *Tzedakah*, equal to the cost of food for one day. One should not leave the *Shul* until the *Sefer Torah* has been returned to the *Aron HaKodesh*.

XII. HILCHOS LIMUD TORAH

1. A male Jew is obligated to study Torah every day and every night for as long as he lives. This *Mitzvah* includes learning *Tenach*, *Talmud*, *Halacha*, *Agadah*, *Medrash* and *Sifrei Mussar*.

2. A woman should learn all about the *Mitzvos* she is obligated to fulfill. Although she is not required to learn Torah, she is rewarded for the Torah she does learn.

3. A father should teach his son *"Torah Tzeevah Lanu Moshe"* (Moshe commanded us to keep the Torah) as soon as the boy is able to speak. The father should also train his son to learn during part of the night.

---

hung heavily upon everyone. "I am no *Choni HaMa'agol*, O Father in Heaven. I have neither his piety nor his wisdom. But your children are in danger, and I cannot be still." He raised his voice and shouted, "Master of the Universe, I swear before You; I shall not leave this circle until rain falls. Almighty G-d, here I stay until You have mercy on your children."

All was still. The people stood expectantly, waiting, waiting. . . . The sun was setting now. The sky was aflame with purple and golden light.

Then someone whispered, "Look, isn't that a cloud?" The whisper was like a shout in the deep silence, as everyone turned to look. Clouds were rolling in faster than I'd ever seen before. The sky darkened as lightning flashed and thunder boomed. The flashes of lightning revealed Grandfather standing perfectly still in his cir-

cle. Only his lips moved.

And then, I felt the first drop.

I've lived for almost eighty years; never again have I felt as I felt then, when the first drops of rain touched my face. The people were overjoyed, embracing and kissing each other—all this while the rain beat down upon them. I didn't stay there. I had to go home with my family to help. Grandfather had fainted.

That is the story of my grandfather and the rain. Following the wonders of that day, we had rain quite often. By the next *Tu B'Shvat* there were colorful street stands again, selling all kinds of fruits.

THE STOLEN VEGETABLES

A Jew stands in prayer before the L-rd but he feels that his heart is empty. He simply cannot concentrate on his prayers. He becomes depressed and feels that all is lost. If he was

59

4. One who cannot study because of intellectual shortcomings should support someone who can study Torah.

5. One should never say, "I will study Torah after I accumulate riches, or when I will have time," because he will then never come to study.

6. One should have a *mokom kovuah* (fixed site) in which to learn.

7. If one is confronted with the decision of either performing a *Mitzvah* for someone else or learning Torah at a specific moment, if no one else is available, he should interrupt his studies to do it.

XIII. LAWS OF MINCHA

1. *Mincha Gedolah* begins 6½ variable hours after sunrise. (A variable hour is calculated by dividing the hours from sunrise to sundown by 12.)

Mincha Ketanoh begins 9½ hours after sunrise.

Peleg HaMincha begins 1¼ hours before sundown.

2. One should *daven Mincha* any time between *Mincha Gedolah* and sunset. Preferably, however, one should *daven Mincha* at a set time every day and should not say *Mincha* early one day and late the next.

3. Even if there was no choice, one can no longer say *Mincha* after *tzais haKochavim* (when the stars appear).

4. From *Mincha Ketanoh* on, one should not do anything (such as eat a big meal) that might cause him to postpone the saying of *Mincha*.

---

unable to concentrate until now, of what value is it to continue—for what can be accomplished with prayers said without feeling?

But this mistake is made clear by the following tale.

A little girl stood in the marketplace selling vegetables at her mother's counter. A drunken peasant started grabbing the vegetables from the counter and the shocked girl began to cry bitterly. A wise man happened to pass by, and he told her:

"Why do you just stand there crying, little fool? There are still some vegetables left. Hurry and grab them and run away. If you don't you won't have any left."

Even if a Jew doesn't succeed in concentrating on more than just a small part of his prayers, he must grab

that opportunity, for if he just gives up, he will lose even that. *(Mishlei Chofetz Chayim)*

BIRCHOS KOHANIM

We only perform the Priestly Blessing on Festivals because Blessings should be given only by those who are joyous of heart, and such rejoicing comes only on Festivals. (Ramah 128:44)

TACHANUN

Tachanun is not recited in the house of a mourner, in the house of a bridegroom, or in the synagogue service when there is a bridegroom in the congregation or when a circumcision is held. This is because in the house of a mourner, the "stern judgment" has already taken place and we do not add to it. As for bridegrooms and the participants in circumcision festivities,

However, one can start a meal at *Mincha Gedolah,* for this will still leave him enough time to complete the meal and also say *Mincha* at its proper time.

5. One should wash his hands before *Mincha,* even if he has been learning Torah during the preceding time.

6. *Mincha* consists of *Ashrei, Shmoneh Esrei, Tachanun,* and *Oleinu.* On fast days, the Torah is read between *Ashrei* and *Shmoneh Esrei.*

XIV. LAWS OF MA'ARIV

1. The preferred time for saying *Ma'ariv* is after *tzais haKochovim* (the appearance of stars in the sky). Opinions vary as to when this takes place, ranging from approximately ½ hour to 72 minutes after sunset. (For the laws regarding the time when *Shabbos* ends, see section on *Shabbos.)*

2. In neighborhoods where it would be difficult to assemble a *Minyan* at a later hour, some have a *Minyan* for *Ma'ariv* at *bain hash'moshos* (twilight), or earlier. In any case, *Ma'ariv* cannot be said before *Pelag HaMincha* (1¼ hours before sunset.) If *Ma'ariv* is said before *tzais haKochovim,* one must repeat the *Shema* later on.

they are in that state of rejoicing which is deemed a time of "mercy" comparable to Shabbos and Festivals, at which time *Tachanun* is not recited. (*Levush* 131:4)

The reasons why the "long" *Ve'hu Rachum* (And He, Being Merciful) is recited on Mondays and Thursdays can be seen from the following story:

V'HU RACHUM

A boat loaded with Jews from Jerusalem landed in a place ruled by a wicked governor. "Where are you from?" asked the governor.

"From Jerusalem," the Jews replied.

"Then I will put you to the test as Chananya, Michoel, and Azaria were tested in the fire." (*Daniel* Ch. 3)

The Jews asked for thirty days grace. They immediately began a fast and whoever had a dream would report it to the others the next morning. At the end of the thirty days, one of the old men, who was very G-d fearing but unlearned said that he had seen in his dream over and over again, a verse which contained the word *"ki"* (when) twice, and the word *"lo"* (not) three times. One of the wise men present, volunteered that the verse must have been *Yeshaya* 43:2 "When you passest through the waters, I will be with you, and through the rivers, they shall not overflow you; when you walk through the fire, you shalt not be burned, neither shall the flame kindle upon you."

"The verse you saw in your dream," the wise man explained, "means that you will be saved from the fire, for you have implicit faith in the promise it contains."

When the governor had the fire lit in the marketplace, the old man walked into the flames and lo and behold the fire separated into three parts and three righteous men were seen enter-

3. If one began to eat a meal before *Ma'ariv*, he may complete the meal and then say *Ma'ariv*. It is best not to start a meal unless one has a set *Minyan* later.

4. One should say *Ma'ariv* before midnight. If midnight passed without his saying *Ma'ariv*, he should say it before *Alos Hashachar*. Once *Alos Hashachar* begins he cannot daven *Ma'ariv* or the *Birchas Krias Shema*, but can still say *Shema*.

5. "*Vehu Rachum*" is said before *Borch*. After hearing *Borchu*, one may not talk.

6. There is no recitation of *Chazoras Ha'Shatz*, or *Tachanun* during *Ma'ariv*.

7. If one arrived late and found the rest of the congregation up to *Shmoneh Esrei*, he should say the *Shmoneh Esrei* with them and say *Krias Shema* and the *Brochos* of *Krias Shema* afterwards.

8. One should make it a fixed practice to learn Torah at night.

9. Before going to sleep, one says *Shema* and the *Brocho* of *HaMapil*. One should not talk or eat after saying *HaMapil*.

---

ing these parts to welcome the old man.

The three righteous ones then began to praise G-d. The first one chanted from "*V'hu Rachum*" to "*Ana Melech*." The second took up the refrain chanting from "*Ana Melech*" to "*En Kamocha*" and the third one took up the refrain from there until the end of the entire prayer.

The Rabbis then decreed that the *V'hu Rachum* should be recited on Monday and Thursdays, which are days of judgment when we plead with G-d for mercy. *(Kol Bo)*

MA'ARIV STORY

The origin of the prayer, "Blessed be the L-rd for ever more . . ." in the *Ma'ariv* service just before the Eighteen *Brochos* can be seen from the following story:

In ancient times the synagogues would be out in the field where there was no human habitation. As a consequence, many people were afraid to stay in the synagogue until after the eighteen *Brochos* were recited because they did not want to walk home through the deserted fields so late. The Rabbis therefore instituted a prayer which is a condensation of the eighteen *Brochos* and in which the name of G-d is mentioned eighteen times. This prayer would take the place of the full *Shmoneh Esrei*. *Kaddish* would then be recited and the people were ready to leave for home. We still observe this custom today because one should not abolish practices sanctified by long-time observance. (*Tur*, Ch. 236; see *Tsofoth Berachos* 4b. sub voce, *de-amar* Rabbi Yochonon)

צִיצִית
Tzitzis

HILCHOS TZITZIS

INTRODUCTION

There is a positive commandment to tie Tzitzis (fringes) on the corners of a garment, as it says (Bamidbar 15), "They should make fringes, on the corners of their clothes." A person should be very careful in the observance of this commandment, since the Torah equates the Mitzvah of Tzitzis to all the other Mitzvos. The Tzitzis symbolize a Jew's willingness to adhere to G-d and His Torah. The word, Tzitzis, in Hebrew, numerically equals 600, which, together with the eight strings and five knots in the Tzitzis, add up to 613, the total number of Biblical commandments. Therefore, by looking at the Tzitzis, one is reminded to fulfill all of G-d's commandments.

TZITZIS

INTRODUCTION

Each fringe of the *Tzitzis* consists of eight threads. The *Talmud (Menachoth* 42a) states: "It is written in the Torah, 'you shall make for thyself twisted cords *(gedillim)* on the four corners of your covering' (*Deut.* 22:12)." Had the word for "cords" been in the singular *(gedil)*, it would have meant that only two threads were needed (as one thread is doubled into two.) The use of the plural form indicates that four threads are required. When these four threads are drawn through the perforation in the garment and then doubled, the result is a total of eight threads. (*Taz* 11:13)

"Rabbi Simon ben Zemach Duran, the *Tashbatz* writes: 'The *Tallis* has four *Tzitzis* (fringes). Since each fringe consists of eight threads, each *Tallis* has a total of thirty-two threads in all, corresponding to the numerical value of the letters in the Hebrew word '*Lev*' (heart)."

THE TALLIS

"Rebbe, lend me your *Tallis* and *Tefillin*, please," asked Avrohom, a simple uneducated Jew. The *Talmidim* of the Rebbe were shocked at the request. They scornfully advised Avrohom that a person must have knowledge before he could pray. However, the Rebbe ignored them and handed Avrohom the *Tallis* and *Tefillin* with a smile. With the *Talmidim* looking on disapprovingly, Avrohom donned the

I. HILCHOS TALLIS KOTON

1. The Torah requires that any male wearing a garment with four or more corners is required to attach *Tzitzis* to each corner. However, the Torah does not require one to don a special four-cornered garment to fulfill this *Mitzvah*. Nevertheless, one who doesn't take advantage of the opportunity to perform this important *Mitzvah* is guilty of acting scornfully towards the *Mitzvos*.

2. The *Tzitzis* must be attached within approximately 2½ inches of each of the corners of a four-cornered garment. However, it must be attached 1¼ inches off the corner of the garment. If the garment became ripped so that the hole of the *Tzitzis* becomes closer to the corners than required, the *Tzitzis* are still kosher. There are two types of garments worn specifically for the purpose of fulfilling this *Mitzvah*. One, often worn under the shirt, is called a *Tallis Koton* (small *Tallis*). Opinions vary as to the measurements of such a *Tallis*, with some requiring a garment of 16x16 inches or 18x18 inches, on both the front and back, and others specifying one of 24x24 inches. Rav Moshe Feinstein, *Shlita*, has ruled that the garment may not be made of synthetic materials, such as nylon or rayon; rather, it must be made of cotton or wool. There are other authorities who disagree.

Tallis and *Tefillin* and went over to the window. Then he gazed outside intently without uttering a sound. Then he quickly took off the *Tallis* and *Tefillin* and without even bothering to refold the *Tallis*, he disappeared.

One of the *Talmidim* quickly went to refold the *Tallis*, and suddenly turned ashen. "What is it?" asked the Rebbe.

"A remarkable thing," stammered the *Talmid* as he held up the *Tallis*. It was dripping wet, as if someone had soaked it in water.

"Amazing," the Rebbe remarked as he took the *Tallis* in hand. "An astounding Jew. Where did he go? We must run after him and find him . . . wonder of wonders."

Quickly they ran after Avrohom and brought him back to the Rebbe.

"How did you get the *Tallis* so wet?" he asked Avrohom. "I have been davening for years, and never did my *Tallis* get so wet. Please tell me your secret."

"Secret? I have no secrets," Avrohom replied. "It's very simple. As I looked out the window, I saw a company of soldiers being drilled, I noticed how they obeyed every order they were given with fear and awe. Why, their bodies practically trembled! I thought to myself: If they shivered so for a drill sergeant who is just a man, how much more should I tremble as I stand before the King of Kings, the Holy One, Blessed Be He!"

"The more I thought about it," Avrohom concluded with artlessness and utter simplicity, "I started to tremble and shake and I found it impossible to

3. The *Tzitzis* themselves are attached to the garment as follows: Four strings are inserted into the hole in each corner of the garment and folded in half, forming eight strings. Each of these strings is composed of thinner single threads ranging from four to eight strands each. One of the strings is specifically made longer than the others. The strings are knotted, and the longest string is wound seven times around the other strings; a double knot is made. The long string is then wound eight times around the others and another double knot is made. This process is repeated twice more, where the long string is wound around the others for eleven and thirteen times, respectively. The number of windings is symbolic, seven, eight, and eleven add up to 26, which is the numerical value of one of the names of *Hashem,* while thirteen is equivalent to the word *"Echod,"* signifying *Hashem's* unity. The *Tzitzis* thus symbolize the words, *"Hashem Echod."*

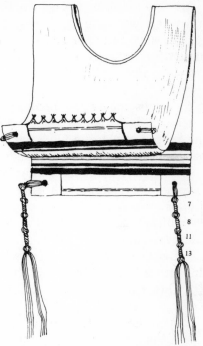

utter a word. A cold sweat broke over me . . . a river of sweat . . . and that is how the *Tallis* became wet."

"But don't worry, Rebbe," continued Avrohom, "it will surely dry soon."

"Who wants it to be dry? Heaven forbid. On the contrary, I seek a way to never let it become dry," answered the Rebbe.

"This story," Reb Yechiel Meir used to say, "led me to Kotzk to learn the '*Y'sod* of *Tefillah*' (the essence of prayer)."

The custom in the household of Reb Yisroel of Ruzhin was to clothe each baby boy in a tiny four-cornered garment fringed with *Tzitzis* from the age of 30 days. It once happened that one of his infant sons—famous decades later as Reb David Moshe of Chortkov—worried his mother by crying without end, refusing to nurse, and being unable to fall asleep despite all her motherly efforts to soothe him. She did not want to call a physician without first telling her husband, but Reb Yisroel only laughed. "Someone has no doubt forgotten to put on the baby's *Tzitzis*" he said. Sure enough, as soon as she placed *Tzitzis* on him he stopped fussing. As a result his

4. The *Tzitzis* themselves must be 12 *godlim* long. (One *godel* is a little less than an inch, with 12 *godlim* being approximately 11 inches.)

5. If one of the strings is torn, the *Tzitzis* remain *kosher*. The same is true when two of the eight strings have been ripped and are less than two *godlim* long, if they are not from the same original string. If this is not known for certain, one should not use the *Tzitzis*. If three of the strings are torn, and are less then two *godlim* long, the *Tzitzis* are *possul* (not valid).

6. *Tzitzis* that were made by machine are *kosher* as long as the machines were manned by Jews who performed the work *lishmoh* (with the proper intent and full knowledge of what they were doing.) Many people prefer wearing hand-made *Tzitzis*.

7. It is preferable that women not make the *Tzitzis*, but if they did so *lishmoh*, the *Tzitzis* are kosher. A child under the age of 13 can make *Tzitzis* as long as he is supervised by an adult who tells him to do it *lishmoh*. *Tzitzis* made by a non-Jew cannot be used since they were not made *lishmoh*.

8. Before putting on the *Tallis Koton*, one should separate and check the strings to make sure that they are *kosher*.

9. One makes the *Brocho* of *"Al Mitzvas Tzitzis"* before putting on the *Tallis Koton*. The *Brocho* is said after the *Brochos* of *"Al Netilas Yodayim"* and *"Asher Yotzar."*

10. While saying *Shema,* one should hold his *Tzitzis* in his left hand,

brothers nicknamed him the *"Tzitzis Jew."*

THE GEMS BY THE ROADSIDE

A certain simple, penniless Jew was blessed with a family of many children, but alas, had no way of providing for them properly. He struggled against hardships in an effort to find work so that he could support himself and his family; but he never succeeded in earning even barely enough.

One day he was walking along the road in bitter despair, since he knew that in his house there was not even enough food for one meal and that there was no prospect in sight of earning any money. As he walked on with his head bowed, he saw a brilliant colored object lying at the roadside— perhaps a piece of broken glass. It was quite certainly nothing to bother about, he thought. It was probably best to keep walking and not waste time over it. Still, he decided, it couldn't hurt to stop and have a look at it. Maybe it had some small value, and he could use it to buy a piece of bread for his children.

He stooped down and picked it up—and could hardly believe his eyes. It was a sparkling polished jewel set in precious metal, and it flashed, glinted and blazed in all the colors of the rainbow as he turned it in his hands.

The man stopped to consider his situation. He was on a main road bet-

but when kissing them he should hold them with both hands.

11. On *Shabbos,* one should be especially careful in checking that his *Tzitzis* meet the required measurements and are not *posul,* for otherwise wearing them may be considered carrying on *Shabbos.*

12. If the corner of the garment was ripped, one cannot resew the garment to place the *Tzitzis* in the required position.

II. TALLIS GODOL

1. The second type of *Tallis* (garment worn specifically to fulfill the *Mitzvah)* is the *Tallis Godol* or large *Tallis.* The *Tallis Godol* can not be so small as to just cover the shoulders; rather, it should be large enough to cover most of the wearer's body. It should be worn with two corners in front and two corners in back.

2. Upon putting on the *Tallis Godol,* one says the *Brocho* of "*Lehisataif Ba'Tzitzis."* This *Brocho* is said while one holds the *Tallis* before him. He then wraps the *Tallis* around the face (until the mouth) and then enwraps himself with it.

3. When someone wears a new *Tallis Godol* for the first time, he says the *Brocho* of *Shehecheyanu.*

4. Married men often cover their heads with the *Tallis Godol* during *Shema, Shmoneh Esrei, Kedusha,* and *Hallel,* while others also do so during *P'sukei D'Zimrah.* One should follow the local custom in this matter.

5. If one removes his *Tallis* or it falls off, he does not have to recite a

ween two towns. Whoever had lost it, had probably lost hope of recovering it, since he was not likely to know where to look for it. Therefore, the jewel was now his. But what sort of precious stone was it? And how much was it worth?

As fast as his legs could carry him, he made for a jeweler in his town. The jeweler examined the stone under his enlarging glass, and whistled in amazement. "I have never seen a gem like this," he said. "It belongs in the king's crown. I will write the royal palace about it, and let's see what happens."

In a short while the king's messengers came to take the poor man and his jewel to the palace. There the king and his advisors examined the stone, and they too were greatly impressed. They found it so beautiful and flawless that they could hardly stop praising it. At last the king called the poor man to him.

"Well, my good fellow," he said, "how much do you want for it?"

The man shrugged his shoulders. "Your majesty, how could I possibly know what price to ask? Until I brought it to the jeweler I did not even know it was valuable."

"Very well," said the king, and at his order the poor man went home a rich man, the owner of a small fortune.

Observant Jews keep the *Mitzvah* of *Tzitzis* with no idea at all of what its

new *Brocho* upon putting it on again, since he is wearing a *Tallis Koton.*

6. The *Tallis* or *Tzitzis* must be worn only during the day, starting from when it is light enough to tell the difference between the white and *Techelles* in the same piece of wool. (Which is the time at which one can recognize his friend at four *amos* away.) The blessing can be made at this time too.

7. A *Tallis Godol* must be shown the proper respect and cannot be worn in the bathroom.

8. We wrap ourselves in the *Tallis* before putting on the *Tefillin* because the *Mitzvah* of *Tzitzis* is so important that the Scriptures equated its observance with the observance of all the commandments in the Bible, as it is written: "That you may look upon them (the *Tzitzis)* and remember all the commandments of the L-rd." (Bamidbar 15:39)

Tallis takes precedence over *Tefillin* since it is put on more frequently than the *Tefillin* which aren't worn on *Shabbos* and *Yom Tov.* "*Todir V'She'Eino Todir, Todir Kodem,*" (In the case that which is frequent, and that which is not as frequent, that which is more frequent takes precedence).

full worth will be to them. They know that Divine reward is promised for keeping the *Mitzvos*—a reward more precious than fine gold and jewels. Yet this is not what they have in mind, because *Mitzvos* have to be observed for their own sake, and not just for a reward. Jews are commanded to pick up every such precious gem that they find by the road of life, without ever really knowing how much or little it may be worth, or how much recompense will be awaiting them in the After-life.

They know that the Divine Sovereign, the supreme King of Kings, can be trusted implicitly. He will pay each and every one faithfully, for every precious gem of a *Mitzvah* that he has observed in his journey through life.

תפילין
Tefillin

INTRODUCTION—TEFILLIN

"And you shall love the L-rd your G-d with all your heart, and with all your soul and with all your might. And these words that I give you today shall be on your heart. . . ."

"And you shall bind them for a sign on your hand and for an insignia between your eyes." (Devorim 6)

This quotation, the beginning of the Shema *prayer, underscores the central position held by the* Mitzvah *of* Tefillin *in the Jewish ritual. When a man wears* Tefillin, *he reaffirms his devotion and love for Hashem and his dedication to His law.*

The Written Torah indicates two distinct types of Tefillin, *and the Oral Torah provides specific details. The two types are the* Tefillin Shel Rosh, *which is placed at the hairline on one's head, and the* Tefillin Shel Yad, *which is put on the biceps of one's arm and whose straps are wound around one's arm, hand, and fingers.*

TEFILLIN

A man should invest time and money in getting proper *Tefillin,* for *Tefillin* serve as a contract of trust between Jews and Hashem. A man drawing up a business contract consults the best lawyers and studies every word of the agreement regardless of how fine the print is. It pays therefore to consult our Torah authorities in order to assure that our contract, the *Tefillin* is in perfect order and that every letter has been written in accordance with the Law.

"Many Jews risked their lives in order to wear Tefillin." (Shabbos 130a)

A SIMPLE JEW'S STORY

I listened, spellbound, as a simple Jew related the trials and tribulations he had suffered in the German concentration camps.

"Did Jews pray in the camps?" I asked suddenly, unable to contain myself in the midst of his account of horrors.

"I prayed daily," he replied firmly.

"But how could you?" I asked in

Each type of Tefillin consists of a square black box called the Bayis. Inside the Bayis is a parchment (or, in the case of the Tefillin Shel Rosh, four parchments) containing four passages from the Torah: the first two parts of Shema, (Devorim 6:4-9 and 11:13-21), the portion of Kadesh (Shemos 13:1-10) and the portion of Vehaya Ki Yi'vyacho (Shemos 13). These passages state a Jew's obligations to Hashem. By wearing Tefillin on his head and on his arm next to his heart, one symbolizes his intention to serve G-d with his thoughts, his feelings, and his every action, and to remember the redemption of the Jews from Egypt.

If a Jew carries out the role presented to him by the message of the Tefillin, he will surely live the type of life required of him. It is no wonder that the Tefillin are so precious a part of Jewish tradition.

HILCHOS TEFILLIN

1. The Tefillin Shel Rosh (of the head) and the Tefillin Shel Yad (of the hand) each contain the above-mentioned four parshios. One set of parshios is put into four separate compartments of the Tefillin Shel Rosh, and the other set is put into the one compartment of the Tefillin Shel Yad.

amazement. "Where did you have Tefillin in the camps? How could you worship with those murderers watching your every move?"

"When your will is strong," he answered shortly, "nothing can stop you." And, never raising his voice, he related:

"As soon as I saw how bad the situation was, I vowed that I would put on Tefillin every day. I never realized how difficult it would be for me to keep the Tefillin from falling into the guard's hands. It was equally impossible to find the time to pray without arousing the Gestapo's suspicions. And yet despite all the difficulties, and though we were under constant guard day and night, we still managed to pray.

"I wasn't the only one," he continued, his voice vibrant with memory. "Jews gathered to pray in every camp. Though we knew quite well that if we would be caught, the penalty would be death, we were hardly frightened. We preferred a death of martyrdom, dying while performing one of G-d's holy precepts, to dying through the slow torture of hunger and hard labor that took so many other lives.

"So now can you understand how I kept my vow, how I never missed one day of prayer with Tefillin?"

"But how strange," I asked in wonder, "that you were never caught?"

"Ah," the simple Jew replied, "but we were. They caught us many times. But somehow or other, I always managed to escape death. One day, I remember, we were instructed not to leave our barracks. To disobey the order meant getting shot. The day passed. It would soon be night, and I still hadn't put on Tefillin that day, for they were hidden in the next barracks. When I realized that it was getting late, I took the risk and sneaked out of my barracks and into the next, where the Tefillin were hidden. I prayed hurriedly, kissed the Tefillin hastily, and

2. There are eight important laws for the making of *Tefillin* which if not observed make the *Tefillin possul* (invalid).

a) The *Battim* (boxes containing the parchment) must be in the shape of a square.

b) The stitches around the *Battim* must be sewn in the shape of a square.

c) All the diagonals of the *Battim* should be equal, making it a perfect square.

d) There should be a figure of a *'shin'* (שׁ) on the right and left sides of the *Tefillin Shel Rosh,* one side having three lines in the *'shin'* and one side four. This *'shin'* must be constructed from the same material as the box.

e) Each *parsha* must be surrounded by a small piece of blank parchment and tied up with animal hair, and then put it into the compartment.

f) The *Tefillin* should be sewn with sinews from a kosher animal.

g) The binding straps should be black.

pushed them quickly back into their hiding place. On my way back to my own barracks I was caught. The Gestapo officer who apprehended me was one of the most vicious in the entire camp. But instead of simply shooting me as I was sure he would, he insisted on knowing where I had gone. He ordered me to tell him why I had risked my life by disobeying the order not to leave the barracks. Realizing that in any event I was lost, I told him that I had gone to pray with the *Tefillin,* that were hidden in the next barracks.

It is still very difficult for me to describe exactly what happened after the SS man heard my explanation. He was like a madman. First he laughed, then he shouted, and then he became very serious and threatened me. "Don't you fool me, you dirty Jew. I want the truth." When I insisted that it was the truth, he tore the sleeve from my left arm, and stood gaping in utter disbelief at the marks left there by the pressure of the *Tefillin* straps.

"So it is true," he roared in fury, and

bursting out again in great peals of uncontrolled laughter, he rushed away.

I was perfectly calm. It was obvious that my end had come.

A great gong sounded, and all the prisoners were herded together in the common yard.

The Gestapo appeared before us menacingly and growled incoherently, "You're all dirty swines," he shouted with disgust. "I never believed that even one of you would be ready to die for his faith. But today I found one." And pointing a claw-like finger at me, he laughed hysterically again and said: "Here he is. From today on, that man is to be allowed to pray in public. No more hiding *Tefillin* and praying in secret."

Lifting a threatening fist to the other guards, he added menacingly, "Whoever makes trouble for him had better watch out."

I refused to believe my ears. It simply was not possible. Then, I realized it must be a miracle. There was

71

h) The knot in the straps of the *Tefillin Shel Rosh* should be tied in the figure of the Hebrew letter *'daled'* (ד). There are various customs as to how this is done.

3. One of the new obligations of one who has become *Bar Mitzvah* is putting on *Tefillin*. This is even more important than being called to the Torah in the synagogue. Wearing the *Tefillin* every day remains a lifelong duty for every Jewish man.

Tefillin are usually put on just before the morning prayers. If one wears a *Tallis*, the *Tallis* is put on before the *Tefillin*. The *Tefillin* should be worn during the entire morning service. In case of a special emergency, where one cannot say the morning prayers, he should put on *Tefillin* anyway. In such a case, one should also try to say the *Shema* while wearing the *Tefillin*.

4. *Tefillin* are never worn at night. Neither are they worn on *Shabbos* or on the festivals mentioned in the Torah, such as *Rosh Hashonoh*,

certainly no other way to explain the incident."

"Did you stay out of trouble after that close call?" I asked, hoping for a reassuring answer from him. Instead he told me another story.

"In one of the camps, we used to pray in the ditches that we dug for the dead. We called these ditches 'the little shul.' One day I was caught while praying there. The S.S. man pulled me out of the ditch while I was still wearing the *Tefillin*. As soon as he realized what I had been doing, he threw me on the ground and began punching and kicking me mercilessly. I was sure that I'd never leave the spot. Finally the guard left me for dead."

"What did you think as you suffered the beating?"

"I can't remember," the simple Jew answered quietly.

"Oh, come now. Surely you had some thoughts," I insisted. "Please think hard; try to remember."

"All right," he said reluctantly. "I'll tell you what I thought. I was in terrible pain. Every bone in my body was aching in pain. All my strength had left me. I felt like a lifeless heap. I knew it was just a matter of time until I joined the other corpses in the ditches. And I remembered some words of *Tehillim*, 'See my pain, and forgive all my sins!' 'See my pain, dear G-d,' I kept repeating in tears, 'See my pain, and forgive me my sins.' I said the words over and over again. And with each word, I felt new strength return, until I pulled myself into the forest, where friends nursed me back to life."

"The man who wears Tefillin is crowned as on high. He enters the perfection of Unity, and so resembles his Creator."

"Tefillin *are called the glory of Israel."* (Succah 25a)

"Rabbah said: 'He who puts on Tefillin *and enwraps himself with* Tzitzis *and says* Krias Shema *and*

Yom Kippur, Succos, Pesach, or *Shavuous.* As to whether one should wear *Tefillin* during *Chol Hamoed* (intermediate festival days), one should follow the custom of his father.

5. Women are not obligated to wear *Tefillin* since it is a commandment observed during a specified time, and not on *Shabbos* and *Yom Tov,* and women are exempt from *Mitzvos* dependent on time *(Mitzvos Asay She'Hazman-gromoh).*

6. The *Tefillin Shel Yad* are put on first. They are worn on the left arm. A completely left-handed person, however, wears them on his right arm. If one is ambidextrous, he puts them on his left arm. If one writes with one hand but does all other work with the other hand, consult a *Rav.* The *Tefillin* is placed on the lower half of the biceps muscle, so that when one holds his arm next to his body, the side of the box should touch his chest. Before tightening the strap, one should say, "I am now about to fulfill G-d's commandment to put on *Tefillin.*" There is also a longer declaration included in most prayer books. One recites the *Brocho* of *Lehani-*

davens *is promised* Olam Habah.' Abaya said: 'The fire of Gehenom will not affect him.' Rav Papa said: 'All his sins are forgiven.'" (Tur Orach Chayim 37)

THE BEST WEAPON OF ALL

During the 1967 War, an Israeli paratrooper was about to parachute into the city of Yerusholayim. Snipers were shooting at the soldiers as they descended, so the paratroopers had to travel very lightly. The paratrooper assembled his backpack with great care. Then he came to his bag of *Tefillin.* He was about to leave it behind on the plane, but then reconsidered, "These *Tefillin* have been with me wherever I've gone," he thought to himself. "Perhaps they will bring me good fortune." Consequently, he put the bag into the backpack as well and then jumped.

The snipers' fire was there to greet him as he landed but he managed to scurry to safety. Later, he examined himself and his belongings. The first thing he removed was his bag of *Tefillin.* Immediately, he noticed a hole in it. He opened it, and found a bullet lodged inside the bag.

"It's a good thing I decided to take my *Tefillin* along," he said to himself. "If I hadn't, that bullet would have penetrated straight through my sack and into my body."

The soldier, and the entire army, had much to be thankful to *Hashem* for, that day.

"The students asked Rabbi Ada ben Ahava: 'Why were you worthy of such long life?' He replied: 'One reason is because I always wore Tefillin.'" (Taanis 20b)

At one time there was a government decree passed declaring that whoever wears *Tefillin* would be killed. Nevertheless, Elisha put his *Tefillin* on and went out with them in public. A government officer saw him and ran after him. When he reached Elisha, the latter had already taken his *Tefillin* off and had put them in his hand.

ach *Tefillin* before tightening the knot of the *Tefillin Shel Yad*. Then the *Tefillin Shel Rosh* are put on immediately after. The strap of the *Tefillin Shel Yad* is wound seven times around the forearm, (sephardim wind it eight times) with the black side of the straps always on the outside. The strap is wound once or twice around the palm of the hand so that it can be held. All these laws go according to custom.

The *Tefillin Shel Rosh* are put on immediately afterwards. One is not allowed to talk or answer anything that is not relevant to putting on the *Tefillin*, until after he has put on the *Tefillin Shel Rosh*. If one does talk then he has to make both *Brochos* on the *Tefillin Shel Rosh*. This should be centered in the middle of the head and worn just over the hairline. It is most important that no part of the box protrudes below the hairline. Although the Torah states that the *Tefillin Shel Rosh* are to be worn "between the eyes", the *Torah She'ba'al Peh* (Orah Torah) explains that this means they should be placed in the middle of the head, above the hairline. If the hairline has receded, then the *Tefillin* should be worn just

The officer said, "What do you have in your hand?"

Elisha replied, "A dove." He opened his hand, and miraculously, a dove flew out into the air.

Thereafter, he was called 'Elisha, The Person with Wings.'

Why did the *Tefillin* appear as a dove? Because *Klal Yisroel* is compared to a dove. Just as a dove's wings protect him, so the *Mitzvos* protect the Jews. (*Shabbos* 49).

"*G-d so loved Israel that He surrounded them with* Mitzvos: Tefillin *on the arm and the head,* Tzitzis *on their garment, and a* Mezuzah *on their door.*" (Menochos 43b)

REB YANKEL MEETS FRANZ JOSEPH

The Austrian Emperor, Franz Joseph, is remembered in Jewish history as one of the few European monarchs who was kind to his Jewish subjects. He was a peace-loving man and believed in justice for all, even the Jews. He treated the Jews as he did any of

his other subjects, and it wasn't long before Jews were playing prominent roles in the affairs of government. This, of course, was resented by other members of the emperor's cabinet, who felt that Jews had no right to partake in the affairs of government. They sought an opportunity to discredit the Jews, and found their chance.

It was customary at that time to have a portrait of the Emperor, Franz Joseph, in all public buildings and houses of worship as a sign of honor and respect to His Majesty. When the emperor went on a tour throughout his kingdom, the plotters saw their chance. While all the Jews of the local community lined the streets waiting to greet His Majesty, they stole the emperor's portrait that was kept in the entrance to the Shul.

The emperor was furious when he walked into the Shul and saw there was no official portrait present. He had been so kind to his Jewish subjects all these years, and yet they

above the point of the original hairline. The knot of the *Tefillin Shel Rosh* must be centered at the base of the skull, in the back of the head, in the indentation. The straps are then allowed to hang in front. Here again, it is most important that the straps be worn with the black side out. Before tightening the straps of the *Tefillin Shel Rosh,* one should say the following blessing: *"Boruch Atoh . . . Al Mitzvas Tefillin."* He should then tighten the straps and say, *"Boruch Shem Kevod Malchuso L'Olom Voed,"* quickly without interruption. Then one completes the windings of the hand *Tefillin* according to custom. (Some do not make any *Brocho*

---

didn't think highly enough of him to display his portrait. His mind was now receptive to all the wicked accusations of his evil ministers.

The Jewish community was thrown into turmoil. No one was brave enough to appear before the emperor to plead for the Jews—no one, that is, except Reb Yankel. He was a poor elderly man who spent his days learning in the *Bais Medrash.* How effective could he be in arguing the Jews' cause? Yet, there was no one else.

An appointment was made for Reb Yankel to appear at the royal court. He dressed in his Shabbos clothes and set out for the palace confident that *Hashem* would help him in his sacred mission.

When Reb Yankel appeared before the emperor, the courtiers were ready to laugh. Was this the best the Jews could do in sending a representative to plead for their very lives?

The emperor knew the reason for this mission so Reb Yankel came straight to the•point. "Your Majesty knows that we Jews pray to G-d every day and always include prayers for the health and welfare of our king and our country. Part of our prayers include the ritual of putting *Tefillin* on our head and on our arm. We do this six days a week as a "sign" of our alle-giance to G-d; *Shabbos,* however, is enough of a sign of allegiance in itself. Therefore, on *Shabbos,* there is no need for the additional sign of *Tefillin.*

"Your Majesty's portrait in our synagogue is a sign all year-round of your subjects' unfailing love and devotion. But on the day that we were honored by your Majesty's royal presence, there was no need for another sign such as a royal portrait."

The members of the royal court stood silent in utter amazement. The Emperor Franz Joseph was impressed by this reasoning. His confidence in the Jews was restored, and until the end of his reign, he remained a steadfast friend of the Jewish people, thanks to the simple Jew named Reb Yankel.

"Man always needs a sign of his bond with G-d. The Shabbos itself is such a sign but on weekdays, this sign is Tefillin." (Eruvin 96a)

"The boxes of Tefillin *represent wisdom, and the straps, the fear of G-d. You can only bind yourself to wisdom through the fear of G-d."*

"He who wears Tefillin . . . *is like one who has built an altar and has offered a sacrifice." (Brochos 15)*

THE TEFILLIN WHICH SHONE
The Sage of Berditchev had lost his *Tefillin* while he was on a visit to a

on the *Tefillin Shel Rosh* but make one *Brocho* before putting it on the arm and thus including the *Tefillin Shel Rosh* as well.) One should go according to the custom of one's father.

7. The three windings around the middle finger symbolize the three-fold bond of love between G-d and Israel. In a sense, they form a threefold wedding ring.

While making these windings, one customarily repeats the following verses from the Book of Hosea (2:21-22).

"V'airastich Lee L'olam. Va'airastich Lee B'tzedek Uvmishpot Uv-chesed Uvrachmim. Va'airastich Lee B'emunoh V'yodaat Es Hashem."

neighboring town. Many of the towns-folk offered him the use of their own *Tefillin* but the Rabbi refused, insisting on praying only with his own.

He sought in vain to buy a new pair, and then the suggestion was made that he should purchase a pair of *Tefillin* from the *Gabbai* of the Shul. In that town there was a tradition to bequeath the *Tefillin* of the deceased to the *Chevra Kadisha*, who later sold them to the synagogue.

The *Gabbai* had hardly set up the array of *Tefillin*, when the Rabbi immediately made his choice. "I'll pay any price for these," he said. The custom of the town was to put the *Tefillin* up for auction, and only the highest bidder could receive them. The *Gabbai* did not want to annul the custom, so he declared an auction. When the people saw the Rabbi's enthusiasm and his willingness to pay any price for this pair of *Tefillin*, they understood that there must be some intrinsic value in them. The price rose to three hundred rubles, and since the *Gabbai* knew that the Rabbi could not pay such a price, he said "This time we are ready to share the cost and give you the *Tefillin* at a small price. Yet we are curious to know why you were so keen on that particular pair without even examining them."

The Rabbi of Berditchev answered, "I shall tell you a story which will show you the value of these *Tefillin*. They belonged to two great men, Rabbi Elimelech and Rabbi Zusha. One day they arrived at a village and lodged in a small inn. The innkeeper was an old man of around eighty years old, and when Reb Zusha saw him, he sighed, "What a pity. This man is eighty years old and still has never laid *Tefillin* in his life."

When the innkeeper heard this he panicked. "How on earth could this be possible? I've been putting on *Tefillin* ever since I was thirteen." He decided to have his *Tefillin* examined. When they were opened it became apparent that there were no scrolls inside. The old man was beside himself and begged the two sages to help him overcome this unforeseen mistake. The pious brothers thought for a moment and then handed him their *Tefillin*. The innkeeper used those precious *Tefillin* with great fervor, only once and then he died. They were automatically passed over to the *Chevra Kadisha*, whose *Gabboim*, not knowing their value put them into the box with all the rest.

"When you opened the box," continued the saint, "I saw a light shining from those very *Tefillin*, and therefore

8. When one removes the *Tefillin*, he reverses the order in which he puts them on. He first unwinds the three coils from the finger, then removes the *Tefillin Shel Rosh*, with the left hand, and finally takes off the *Tefillin Shel Yad*. The *Tallis* is removed after the *Tefillin*.

9. The *Tefillin* should always be shown the reverence due a sacred object, especially while one is wearing them. One should not engage in idle conversation while wearing *Tefillin*.

10. The *Tefillin Shel Rosh* should not be worn without the *Tefillin Shel Yad*. However, if one has no arms, or is otherwise unable to put *Tefillin* on his arm, he should put on the *Tefillin Shel Rosh* anyway.

11. One should touch his *Tefillin* from time to time so that he does not take his mind off them for a second. It is a custom to kiss the *Tefillin* when putting them on and taking them off.

I wanted only them."

"*It is written, 'Behold you are beautiful My love.' The beauty of Israel before G-d is* Tefillin." (Shir Hashirim)

RABBI LEVI YITZCHOK

It is told that the saintly Rabbi Levi Yitzchok of Berditchov once saw a simple Jew drop his *Tefillin*. The man gently lifted them up and lovingly kissed them. The Rabbi then raised his hands and said, "L-rd of the universe. The Jewish people are Your *Tefillin*. You have dropped them and let them lie on the ground for more than two thousand years, trampled by their enemies. Why do You not pick them up? Why do You not do as much as the most simple Jew? Why?"

"*When a man wears* Tefillin, *a voice proclaims to all the angels of the chariot who watch over prayer, 'Give honor to the image of the King, the man who wears* Tefillin." (Zohar 55 124a)

"*The light of* Tefillin *illuminates the holiness of the Land of Israel.*"

"*The* Tefillin *straps encompass your faith, protecting it from the Outside Forces. When your mind and soul are thus safeguarded, you can attain a perception of the innermost light.*"

(Lekutey Etzos, Tefillin 1)

בְּרָכוֹת

Brochos

BROCHOS

INTRODUCTION

Everything in this world is considered as if it is hekdesh *(sanctified), as the* posuk *states, "L'Hashem Ha'Oretz U'M'Loah"* (the earth and everything in it belongs to G-d). *Just as one is not permitted to have any benefit from an item that is* hekdesh *without first redeeming it, so one is not permitted to have any benefit from anything in this world without first redeeming that item. With foods and fragrant odors, this is accomplished through the* Brocho Rishono *(blessing before using the item). Making a* Brocho Rishono, *in a sense, is like asking permission from G-d to use the item.*

Brochos (blessings) serve to remind us that Hashem *is the source of all good fortune and sustenance, and they give us the opportunity to thank Him for His good will.*

BROCHOS

ONE HUNDRED BROCHOS

Rabbi Meir said that a person is obliged to recite a hundred blessings every day as it is said, "What does Hashem your G-d ask of you? (*Deut.* 10:12). Instead of '*Mah*' ('what'?), read '*Ma'oh,*' a hundred." (*Menachos* 43b)

The reason we recite at least 100 Brochos each day is because during the days of the Jewish kings, 100 Jewish people died daily. No one knew the reason for this until King David came to understand that it was because the people were not giving thanks to G-d for all the goodness and kindness He had shown them. David therefore,

instituted the one hundred Brochos to offset the 100 deaths, and as soon as people began to recite the 100 Brochos each day, the dying ceased. Another reason for saying at least 100 Brochos daily is to counteract the 99 curses found in the Book of Devorim: 98 in Devorim 28:15-58, and 1 more in Devorim 28:61. (*Tur, Simon 46, Orach Chaim*)

The Chidushei Harim comments that the hundred daily blessings are comparable to the hundred silver sockets which held up the walls of the Mishkon (desert tabernacle) (*Shemos* 38:27). Just as the abode of G-d's holiness on earth is supported by man-

HILCHOS BROCHOS

A. One is required to say a *Brocho Rishono* before eating even the slightest amount of food.

B. One should hold the item in his or her right hand at the time of saying the *Brocho*. He should also have the proper *kavono* (intentions) when saying the *Brocho*. Also, he should be aware of the *Brocho* he will be saying, before he starts the *Brocho*.

C. There are several different *Brochos* over food, depending on the character of the food. *Ha'Motzee* is said over bread; *Ha'Gofen*, over wine products; *Mezonos*, over foods made from grain (like cake); *Ho'Etz*, over fruits grown on a tree; *Ho'Adomoh*, over foods grown from the ground; and *She'Hakol* over other foods.

1. *She'Hakol* is recited over fruits and vegetables that are so unripe as to be sour and unappetizing, or which are raw and are not usually eaten raw (e.g. potatoes, onions). If a fruit or a vegetable is mashed or processed until the original form of the food can no longer be recognized, a *She'Hakol* is said, unless the usual method of processing the food is to mash it and change it to a different form.

2. If bits and pieces of the food are in its original form and are still visible, such as in the case of homemade applesauce, the original *Brocho* (in this case *Ho'Etz*) is said. If the vegetable was just sliced and processed (not mashed), even if it is unrecognizable, it still retains its original *Brocho*. Examples of this are potato chips which require *Ho'Adomoh*, and corn flakes (rolled not mashed) which are also *Ho'Adomoh*. Mashed potatoes almost always require *Ho'Adomoh*.

Ho'Adomoh is recited on soup made from vegetables cooked in

made silver sockets, so too, the recognition of His presence on earth requires man's daily recitation of blessings.

The blessing is man's recognition that the earth and its fullness are G-d's. Man was put on earth to acknowledge that fact. Once he has done so, the earth belongs to him. Having utilized G-d's gifts to realize that the earth is G-d's alone, man is granted the right to make use of G-d's possession.

There is another interpretation of 'blessing'. It is expounded by the Rashba *(Tshuvos* 5:51) and expounded upon by the *Nefesh Hachaim* (2:1-4). The word 'Brocho', blessing, is derived from 'Breicha', a spring. Just as a spring flows constantly, always producing fresh supplies of water, so G-d is the source of infinite blessing. In creating the universe with its inhabitants, it was His desire to establish the conditions that would enable Him to do good to others.

"I will bless the L-rd at all times; his praise shall continually be in my mouth." (Tehillim 34: 2)

"Bless the Lord, O my soul, and

water, and on cooked vegetables. Fruit soup with fruit in it requires
Ho'Etz. If the fruit is removed, *She'Hakol* is said, unless the usual
method of processing this fruit is by cooking.

3. All juices that are extracted from fruit are *She'Hakol,* except for
wine, which is *Ha'Gofen. Ha'Gofen* is also recited over wine mixed with
water, unless there is six times as much water as wine. (Most wines have
water already added, so the amount in these cases is less than six.) If
wine is mixed with beer, and there is more beer than wine, *She'Hakol* is
recited.

4. Berries that grow on a tree require *Ho'Etz.* Berries that grow on
bushes whose stem disappears in the winter require *Ho'Adomoh.* e.g.
blueberries, bananas and raspberries.

5. If one derives pleasure from the taste of medicine, it is questionable
whether he should make a *Brocho* on it. Water taken to facilitate the
swallowing of pills or medicine does not require any *Brocho.* If fruit juice
or any other drink is used for this purpose, a *Brocho* must be made.

6. If a soup is made by cooking meat and vegetables, *She'Hakol* is
recited over the mixture, because the meat taste in the soup is the
dominant taste. An example of this is chicken soup. However, if the
vegetables are eaten with the soup only *Ho'Adomoh* is made. An example of this is a bean soup flavored by meat or bones. If the meat is also
served with the soup, two *Brochos* should be made.

7. In case two foods are combined to form one dish, such as in a
casserole, soup or cocktail, then if one food is clearly the main ingredient
(ikor) and the others are just there to flavor it, or bind it together *(toffel)*
then the only *Brocho* made is the one on the *ikor,* even if the *ikor* is the

all that is within me, bless His holy
name; Bless the Lord O my soul
and forget not all His benefits."
(Tehillim 103:1-2)
The benedictions are all worded
in the present tense to show that all
things are in constant process of creation, as we recite in our prayers, "In
His goodness He continually renews
the act of Creation every day" (Daily
Prayers). G-d is the prime cause of the
Universe and without Him there would
be no life. As Creator of the Universe,
He is constantly at work creating and
recreating in accordance with His will.
(Sefte Emeth, by the Rebbe of Brezan)

The reason why wine requires a
Brocho of its own, rather than the
regular *Brocho* recited over other fruit
juices is because it is the change from
grape juice to wine that makes this
fruit important, for wine gladdens the
heart. (*Brochos* 35b)

When wine is drunk and the blessing *Borei Pri Hagefen* is recited no
other blessing need be recited over
any other beverages served with the
meal, providing that the other beverages were served at the time when the
benediction over the wine was made.
This is because wine is an important
beverage for which a distinct *Brocho*

smaller ingredient. A typical case is a jam where, though sugar may be 80% of the mixture, the *Brocho* is nonetheless made on the fruit. In the case of no clear-cut *ikor*, the food constituting the greatest part of the mixture is considered the *ikor*. In case *Mezonos* material is part of the mixture (wheat, etc. not rice) in a minor amount, it is always considered the *ikor*, unless it is just there to (a) bind the food together, (b) thicken it, (c) color it, or (d) form a glaze.

If a cracker is used merely as a tool to hold a mixture (such as chopped liver) which cannot be grasped by the fingers, no *Brocho* is required on the cracker, even if eaten together with the mixture. Similarly, a flavorless ice-cream cone requires no *Brocho* when eaten together with the ice cream, primarily to hold the ice cream. Only *She'Hakol* is made in this case. However, if the cone or cracker is eaten by itself or for its own taste, two *Brochos* are required.

8. If someone made a *Brocho* of *Ho'Adomoh* over a food which requires a *Ho'Etz*, he is *yotzai* (fulfilled the requirement). If someone made a *Ho'Etz* over a food which requires a *Ho'Adomoh*, he is not *yotzai*. If one makes a *She'Hakol* over any food (including fruits, vegetables, wine and bread), he is *yotzai*.

9. One must make a *Brocho* even if he intends to eat only a small amount of food. However, one need not make a *Brocho* if he is tasting food (e.g., to see if the food had enough salt), even if he swallows a small amount in this way. Preferably, one should intend to eat the food for its own sake in such an instance and make a *Brocho*.

10. One should remove all inedible portions of the food (such as peels and shells) that make it hard for him to eat the food, before reciting the *Brocho*.

of its own has been prescribed. There are many occasions when one must pronounce a benediction over wine, even if he has no desire to drink it, e.g. for *Kiddush, Havdalah,* the marriage ceremony etc. Therefore all other beverages served after wine are considered of less importance, and do not require the recital of a new blessing. (*Brochos* 41b; *Levush* 174:4; *Taz* and *Magen Avrohom* 174:1-2)

AMEN

Many years ago there lived in Spain an eminent Torah scholar of saintly character. This man enjoyed a very close friendship with the king who appreciated his wisdom and often sought his advice on matters of state.

The king's priest, who hated all Jews, detested this Jew particularly because of the honor the king bestowed on him. He plotted constantly to embitter the lot of the Jewish community. From time to time the king, under the priest's malevolent influence would issue evil decrees against the Jewish people, but each time, the king's friend, through his Torah wis-

11. If one talked between the recitation of the *Brocho* and the eating of the food, he should repeat the *Brocho*. However, if there was merely a long pause before eating, and one did not interrupt his trend of thought in regard to the food, he need not repeat the *Brocho*. After making a *Brocho*, one should not answer *Omein* to someone else's *Brocho* before he has eaten.

12. If one will be served several types of food requiring the same *Brocho* he should intend that the *Brocho* should cover all of the foods requiring this *Brocho*. Thus, even in certain cases where a new *Brocho* might be required for additional food served, his deliberate intention at the beginning spares him from making a new *Brocho*. In any case, if one had decided not to eat anything else and then changed his mind, a new *Brocho* is required. When one eats at someone else's table, he need not make new *Brochos* on each new food, since he had in mind to eat all food the host will serve him.

13. If one drank wine and had other liquids on the table, if he had in mind to drink other liquids, or if he intended to make a meal of the wine, then he does not have to make a separate *Brocho* on other liquids which he drinks. All this applies if at least 2 ounces of wine was drunk.

14. If one has many different foods before him he makes the *Brochos* in the following order: a) *Mezonos* b) *Gafen* c) *Ho'etz* d) *Ho'Adomoh* e) *She'Hakol*.

BROCHO ACHRONOH

Just as one must make a *Brocho* before one eats, so, too, must one make a *Brocho* afterwards to thank *Hashem* for the food which *He* has given him.

dom and saintliness, was able to persuade the king to annul them. This infuriated the hateful priest, and he decided to concoct some false charge to be permanently rid of the Jew.

He found the opportunity he was waiting for when the king, in desperate need of funds, permitted himself to be persuaded to issue an edict banishing all Jews and forfeiting their property to the crown.

The leaders of the community once again called on the king's friend and asked him to intercede with the monarch to annul this decree.

When he arrived at the palace, the king as always greeted his Jewish friend very graciously. This lifted the latter's spirits and he interpreted it as a sign that this time too, he would be able to persuade the king to withdraw the edict. Meanwhile, some very prominent personages arrived, including the anti-Semitic priest, and they engaged the king in a lengthy conversation.

Realizing that he had not yet davened *Mincha*, the afternoon service, and noticing that the king was occupied with his other guests, the king's

1. After most foods, the *Brocho Achronoh* of *"Borei Nefoshes"* is said. There are several exceptions:

2. a) The *Brocho Achronoh* of *"Al Hamichya"* is said after foods made of one of the "five types" of grain, (wheat, barley, oats, rye and spelt). b) The *Brocho* of *"Al Hagefen"* is said after wine. c) The *Brocho* of *"Al Ho'etz"* is said after the five fruits that *Eretz Yisroel* is famous for (grapes, figs, pomegranates, olives and dates).

These complete *Brochos* can be found in the *Siddur*. There is one variation omitted from most *Siddurim*. In the ending of the *Brocho* after the five fruits, *"Al Ho'Oretz V'Al HaPeiros"* changes to *"V'Al Peiroseho"* when the fruit was grown in *Eretz Yisroel*. (One says *Borei Nefoshos* on rice, even though the *Brocho Rishono* is "Borei Meenei Mezonos.")

3. If one drank wine and also ate grapes, he must mention *"Al Ho'Etz"* in the *Brocho Ach'ronoh,* in addition to *"Al Hagefen."*

4. If someone ate cake, drank wine, and then ate grapes, he says, *"Al Hamichya," "Al Hagefen"* and *"Al HaPeiros,"* all in one *Brocho*.

5. If someone ate one of the *Shiva Minim* (seven fruits of Israel) which are wheat, barley, grapes, figs, pomegranates, olives, and dates, and then ate additional fruits not from the *Shiva Minim,* he need not make a *Borei Nefoshos* on the other fruits, for the *Al Ho'etz* includes them. However, if one ate one of the *Shiva Minim,* and then drank fruit juice, he must make a separate *Borei Nefoshos* on the juice. Similarly, if one ate a piece of cake and a fruit not from the *Shiva Minim,* then he must recite both *"Al Hamichya"* and *"Borei Nefoshos."*

6. If one eats less than a *kezayis* (size of an olive) of food within four to nine minutes, or drinks less than a reviyis (3.3-4.4 oz.) within a minute, he need not say a *Brocho Ach'ronah* afterward.

Jewish friend walked over to a corner of the room to *daven*. This was what the priest had been waiting for. Quickly, he stood up and announced in hushed tones that he was about to bestow a blessing upon the king, and emphasized that all present must answer Amen at its conclusion. Naturally, every person in the room answered Amen after the blessing except the lone figure in the corner who was still engrossed in prayer and was not aware of what was going on. Suddenly the priest's face assumed an expression of deepest anguish. Lifting his hands to his head, he screamed that the Jew, by not answering Amen, had destroyed the effect of his blessing. Turning to the king, he sneered, 'And this is your loyal Jewish friend on whom you dote so?' The king was unable to reply and in a fit of uncontrollable fury, ordered that his Jewish friend be hacked to pieces and all Jews deported from his land. The order was swiftly carried out.

The frightful fate of the great *Tzaddik* had a demoralizing effect upon the

GENERAL LAWS ON BROCHOS

1. If someone made the wrong *Brocho* on any item and corrected himself within *Toch K'dei Dibbur* (within the amount of time necessary to say three words, *"Sholom Aleichem, Rebbe")* of the ending of the erroneous *Brocho,* it is considered a valid *Brocho.*

2. One should refrain from eating a complete pitted fruit which is smaller than a *kezayis* as some authorities require a *Brocho Ach'ronah* to be made in this case. If one is uncertain as to whether he ate a *Kezayis,* he should not make the *Brocho Ach'ronah.*

3. If one is uncertain as to whether he made a *Brocho Rishona* or *Ach'ronah,* he need not make a new *Brocho,* except in the case of *Birchas HaMazon.*

4. One says *Birchas HaMazon* after having eaten a *kezayis* of bread. The saying of *Birchas HaMazon* removes the obligation of making all *Brochos Ach'rono* over other foods eaten during the meal. On occasion, though, one does have to make separate *Brocho Rishonos* during a meal, such as on desserts and wine.

5. In general, one should be careful not to eat any foods immediately before washing for a meal with bread, for this would cause him to make unnecessary *Brochos.*

6. If one made a *Brocho* intending to eat meat during the nine days between *Rosh Chodesh Av* and the Ninth of *Av* (during which time the eating of meat is prohibited), and then he realized that eating meat is improper, he should nevertheless eat a small amount of the meat so as not to have made a *Brocho L'vatoloh* (unnecessary Brocho) unless he intended to eat something else on the table for which the *Brocho* is *She'Hakol.*

Jews of Spain. The Rabbi of that community was especially shocked. A close friend of the martyr, he knew him to be a truly G-d fearing man, thoroughly observant of all *Mitzvos.* He could not help wondering what he had done to deserve such a grisly, untimely end. Not that he doubted for a moment the justice meted out in heaven; he was absolutely certain that G-d is just and His judgment is correct. Nevertheless, he was extremely anxious to learn the nature of the sin of which his friend was guilty so that he could warn others to guard against it. He engaged in much fasting and prayed that this secret be revealed to him.

In answer to his prayers, the martyr appeared to him in a dream and said to him: "Fear not, I came to tell you why so terrible an edict was issued against me. Of the saintly, G-d expects the very highest standard of obedience, for they set the example which others follow.

I was once guilty of a grave sin: I failed to answer *Omein* when my little son recited a *Brocho.* As G-d is com-

7. One is prohibited from using *Hashem's* name in vain, or from erasing or destroying writing containing *Hashem's* name. However, one is allowed to erase a tape recording containing *Hashem's* name (such as in the case of a recording of Torah *laining*) because such a recording is not considered writing. There are those who disagree. Therefore, one should take care not to record the properly pronounced name of *Hashem* unless one intends to preserve the tape.

OTHER BROCHOS

I. BORAI MEENAI BESOMIM:

1. Various blessings are recited on fragrant smells from natural sources, but not on deodorants, perfumes or cleansers.

2. The *Brocho* should be recited before one actually smells the fragrance. If one accidentally smelled the fragrance before reciting the *Brocho* he should not recite the *Brocho* afterwards, unless he plans to smell the fragrance again.

3. The *Brocho* of *"Borai Atzai Besomim"* is recited over a fragrance emanating from a tree, while the *Brocho* of *"Borai Isvai Besomim"* is said over a fragrance coming from any type of grass or flowers. If one is uncertain as to the source of a fragrance, or if the fragrance comes from an animal source, or is compounded from various sources requiring different *Brochos*, he should say *"Borai Meenai Besomim"*.

4. If a fruit has a sweet fragrance and can also be eaten, one should recite the *Brocho* of *"Hanosen Rayach Tov BePeiros."* If his only intention was to eat the fruit, and he only smelled it inadvertantly, no *Brocho* is made on the smell.

---

passionate, I was not punished immediately. Instead, He waited until I again failed to answer Amen after the priest's blessing. Here, as the Heavenly Tribunal again considered my sin, *Satan* testified against me: If it is considered so great a sin not to answer Amen to a blessing for a flesh-and-blood king, how much greater is the sin of not answering Amen to a blessing for the King of Kings. Then and there my fate was sealed for my first sin—for not answering Amen to my son's *Brocho.*

"And now, my dear friend," continued the martyr, "tell my story to your family as well as to all people. Warn them to be ever most alert to answer *Omein.* It is very unfortunate that so many are so careless in fulfilling this *Mitzvah."*

"The 'Amen' uttered when a blessing is heard is a sort of acquiesence in the benediction uttered, and is therefore an integral part of it. Consequently, just as the words of the blessing are to be said with devotion and concentration, the brief 'Amen' too is to be uttered with seriousness and solemnity."

5. No *Brocho* is made upon smelling or inhaling tobacco. It is questionable whether one should make a *Brocho* upon smelling an *Esrog* on *Succos*, and he, therefore, should not smell the *Esrog* by itself until after *Succos* when the *Brocho* "Hanosen Rayach Tov BePeiros" is made.

II. TEFILLAS HADERECH:
One says *Tefillas HaDerech* (travelers prayer) when traveling a distance from the city. It is recited immediately upon departing from the city. One should not say *Tefillas HaDerech* more than once a day during a long trip, even if several trips are made during one day. A Rav should be consulted as to the law when one stops often between trips. If one forgot to say *Tefillas HaDerech* until the trip was almost over, then he should say it without a *Brocho*.

III. BIRCHAS HAGOMEL:
1. One must say *Birchas Hagomel* (Blessing of Thanks) after one of the following occasions: (a) Returning from a potentally dangerous trip; (b) Crossing a sea or ocean; (c) Recovering from a dangerous illness; (d) Being released from prison; (e) Being saved from any deadly situation.

2. Rav Moshe Feinstein, Shlita, is of the opinion that one must say *Birchas HaGomel* after taking any airplane trip, even if it is a very short one; others say that this is necessary only if one crossed the ocean during the trip. If the trip involves several different stops, one should say *Birchas HaGomel* only after the final stop.

3. Women and children should not say *Birchas HaGomel*. Instead, the husband or father should include them in his own *Birchas HaGomel* if he was in the same situation. If not, consult your *Rav*.

"We are supposed to respond Amen to each Brocho that we hear because it is written, 'For I will proclaim the name of the L-rd, Ascribe ye Greatness unto our G-d.' (Deut. 32:3) Also, Moshe said to Israel: 'When I will recite a Brocho, you shall answer Amen.' (Abudraham) The initials of El Melech Ne'eman ('G-d Faithful King') are also the initials of Amen. (Rabbi Haninah-Sabbath 119b; see Tur, Ch. 124)

"Rabbi Shimon ben Lakish said: "He who responds Amen with great fervor will have the gates of Eden opened for him, as it is written, 'Open the gates, that there may enter the righteous nation, which guards the truth'. (Yeshaya 26:2) Read not 'Shomer Emunim' (which guards the truth), but 'She'Omrim Amen' (which say amen)." (Shabbos 119b)

MAYIM RISHONIM
During the time of the Talmud, there were times when Jews in business did not want it known that they were Jewish. One such person was an innkeeper who sold both Kosher and non-Kosher meat.

4. One should say *Birchas HaGomel* within three days of the incident. However, if the three days have already elapsed, he can still recite *Birchas HaGomel*, until 30 days have passed. This is usually done after one has been called to the Torah, in the company of at least ten men. If one recites *Birchas HaGomel* with the intention of including someone else who is listening, both are *yotzai*.

IV. SHE'HECHIYANU:

1. One recites the *Brocho* of *She'hechiyanu* as a special *Brocho* to praise *Hashem* for the joy of new things. These include: a) eating a fruit for the first time during the year, b) when wearing important new clothes for the first time, c) upon seeing one's baby daughter for the first time. ("*Hatov Vehameitiv*" is said when being notified of the birth of a son.) d) at the beginning of *Yomim Tovim*, e) after building or buying a new house, or, f) after new *Mitzvos*.

2. The *She'hechiyanu* on new fruits is recited only on fruits that do not grow throughout the entire year. One does not say a *She'hechiyanu* on new grapes if he drank wine from the same season beforehand or vice versa. It is questionable whether one makes a *She'hecheyanu* upon eating a nectarine if he has already eaten a peach or a plum. Only one *Brocho* is made over a mixture of various new fruits. Some say *She'hechiyanu* before the *Brocho* of *Ho'Etz*, while others say it afterwards.

3. If one demolished his house and rebuilt it as originally, he does not make *She'hechiyanu*, nor does he make *She'hechiyanu* if he sold his house and bought it back. If he rebuilt his house after it was demolished by fire, he makes *She'hechiyanu*. Partners who built or bought a house

If a man walked in and washed his hands before eating, the innkeeper knew he was Jewish and served him Kosher meat. If, on the other hand, he did not wash before sitting down to the meal, the owner knew that he was not a Jew.

It happened one time that a man sat down without washing his hands. As was his custom in such a situation, the innkeeper gave the man *treifa* (non-Kosher) meat. After the meal, the man wanted to pay and was surprised to hear the high cost of the meat.

"Well, you had ham," answered the innkeeper, "and it's more expensive."

The man grew excited and started to yell. "But I am Jewish. How dare you serve me ham?"

The innkeeper answered apologetically, "I have no way of knowing who is Jewish and who is not, except by whether or not someone washes before a meal. So when I saw you come in and sit down immediately to eat without washing before you ate the bread, and without saying a blessing, I assumed you were a gentile."

From this incident our *Chachomim* (Sages) said: Because of lack of *Mayim Rishonim* (washing before eating bread at the beginning of a meal), a Jew

make *"Hatov Vehameitiv"* (the *Brocho* made when a good experience is shared by more than one person). The same applies to a *Shul* or public building.

V. MISCELLANEOUS BROCHOS:

1. If one sees a close relative after a year's separation, during which time he did not receive any information about him, he says the *Brocho* of *"Mechayei Ha'Meisim,"* although this is done very rarely.

2. Upon learning of the death of a close relative, one recites the *Brocho* of *"Boruch . . . Dayan Ho'Emess."* If one learns of the passing of one who was not a relative, he says *"Boruch Dayan Ho'Emess,"* without saying the name of *Hashem*.

3. If one sees a non-Jewish king, he says the *Brocho* of *"She'Nosan Michvodo L'Bossor Vodom."* However, this does not apply to a President or any elected official because their powers are not permanent.

4. The *Brocho* to be said upon seeing lightning is *"Oseh Ma'Aseh Beraishis,"* and that upon hearing thunder is *"SheKocho U'Gevuroso Molai Olom."* The former is said first, for lightning precedes thunder. One should not say these more than once during a rain storm, and one should say them *Toch K'dei Dibbur*.

5. One says the Brocho of *"Oseh Ma'Aseh Beraishis"* upon seeing unusual occurrences, such as earthquakes, tornadoes, and meteors, and for *Birchas Hachama* (blessing of the sun) which is said once every 28 years. The next time it is scheduled on the calendar is the Jewish year 5769 (secular year 2009).

---

ended up eating *treifa* meat. (*Chulin* 106a)

"And you shall take good care of your bodies." (Devorim 4)

"Our eating and drinking are hallowed by the benedictions and the washing before and after the meal. Failure to observe the custom of the washing before meals led ultimately to the eating of pork; failure to wash the hands after the meal led to the slaying of a person." "Whoever makes light of washing the hands (before and after a meal) will be uprooted from the world." (Sotah 4)

"Whoever makes light of wash-

ing the hands (before the meal) will become poor." (Shabbos 62b)

FOOD IS NOT FOR WASTING

Babylonia had a very fruitful year. The rains were abundant and the earth yielded a rich harvest. Flour was plentiful and bread was cheap. People became careless. They threw away the leftovers, and they wasted their bread. Food became a plaything to them.

One day, two people were standing in the marketplace and throwing bread at each other in sport. At that moment a wise man named Rabbi Yehuda passed by. When he saw the people playing around with bread and abus-

6. One should also say *"Oseh Ma'Aseh Beraishis"* upon seeing beautiful sites for the first time, e.g. the Grand Canyon, which inspires one to appreciate Hashem's greatness.

7. One says the Brocho of ". . . *Zocher HaBris"* upon seeing a rainbow.

8. Once a year, when one sees blossoming fruit trees in the spring, the *Brocho* of *"Shelo Chisar Be'Olomo Klum etc."* is recited. This applies to the flower and not the leaves. The *Brocho* can only be made in the first month of the spring season. Once the fruit comes out, no *Brocho* can then be made. Only one such *Brocho* is made per year.

ing their food, he stopped in indignation.

"It appears that we have too much food," said Rabbi Yehuda angrily. "People are so satisfied that they have forgotten the commandment of the L-rd: Do not destroy! Do not waste food! If that is the case, then it would be well to have famine in the land, so that people will appreciate the food G-d grants them."

Rabbi Yehuda was a righteous man, and G-d made his words come true. There was no rain the next year and nothing grew. No wheat or barley appeared, and no vegetables were available. The little food which was left over from the year of plenty was scarce and expensive. People waited in long lines to buy their bread. Some went hungry and as they suffered, they remembered with sadness and regret how they had wasted their food when they had plenty. "We wish that we now had just a little dry bread," they moaned. moaned.

Rabbi Yehudah did not know about the trouble that had come to the world, for he was accustomed to sitting at home all day and studying Torah, and he rarely went outside. The other sages saw the people suffering and said to Rav Kahana, Rabbi Yehuda's helper, "You are always in the company of the righteous man, Rabbi Yehuda. Arrange for him to go to the marketplace so that he can see how hungry the people are."

Rav Kahana agreed and asked Rabbi Yehudah to come out with him. When they reached the marketplace, they saw a great many people standing in line near the platform of the only merchant in the entire marketplace.

Rabbi Yehdah was surprised. "What is this? Why are so many people gathered here?" he asked in wonder.

"This is the only merchant who has food to sell. And all he has are meager leftovers and peels of dates. It is worthless food, and yet the hunger is so great that everyone is anxious to buy some of it," the people said.

"The famine has indeed come to the world," said Rabbi Yehuda. "If that is so, we must proclaim a fast day—a day of atonement. We must pray to G-d for mercy. We must ask G-d to give food to hungry people."

He then turned to his servant and said, "Please take off my shoes." (On the major fast days of *Yom Kippur* and *Tisha B'Av*, we do not wear shoes.)

The servant had barely managed to take off one shoe, when it began to rain. As soon as Rabbi Yehuda started to pray, the rain fell in torrents. That is because G-d instantly fulfills the wishes

סעודה וברכת המזון
Seudah and Birchas Hamazon

LAWS OF WASHING FOR A MEAL

I. REASONS AND CONDITIONS:

1. One washes his hands before eating bread to sanctify ourselves like the *Kohanim*, who washed their hands before eating *Terumah* (the portion of produce given by the people to the *Kohanim*). In addition, washing is a method of purification and cleanliness.

2. One should wash with a *Brocho* only before eating at least the size of a *Beitzoh* (egg) of bread. One washes without a *Brocho* before eating any foods which are usually dipped into the following liquids: 1) water 2) dew 3) milk 4) oil 5) wine 6) honey and eaten with the hands. This includes corn with melted butter. However, if the food is dry or is eaten only with utensils like a spoon or a fork, washing is not required. Washing is not required before drinking liquids.

II. METHOD:

1. When someone washes his hands, he must use a cup that can hold a *Reviyis* of water. The person must pour the water over his hands through the power of a person *(Koach Gavra)*; he cannot simply place his hands under an open tap, even if it comes from a utensil such as a barrel.

---

of a righteous man for the good of mankind.

Very soon, the crops were growing again, and the famine ceased. The people ate and thanked G-d for His gracious kindness. Now they fully appreciated it.

"The ill-mannered is not only despised, but is not even considered a reliable and responsible person. Our Rabbis taught, 'He that eats in the marketplace is like a dog; and some say that he is unfit to testify (for he lacks self respect).' " (Kiddushin 40b)

"He who eats before his guest (without inviting him to join) is to be condemned."

"Said R. Yochanan: 'Don't talk when you eat lest the food go down the wrong way and you choke.' " (Taanis 5b)

"Do not talk while you eat." (Taanis 5b)

2. One takes the cup in his right hand and fills it with water. He then transfers the cup to his left hand and pours the water two times over his right hand. The same is repeated for the left hand. The water should reach the wrist, but if not enough water is available, washing until the knuckles is sufficient.

3. One who has just come from the bathroom and intends to wash for a meal, should first wash his hand in a manner unfit for *Netilas Yodayim*, make the *Brocho* of *Asher Yotzar*, and then wash properly for *Netilas Yodayim*.

4. Before washing, one must remove from his hands all objects that may keep the water from reaching part of his hands. These are called *chatzitzos*, and include rings and bandages. If one cannot remove a bandage, he should pour at least a *Reviyis* of water over the hand. Certain ink or cement is considered a *chatzitzoh* unless its presence results from a person's profession (e.g., if one is a printer or painter). However, even if one's profession does cause his hands to become dirty, the dirt should not cover most of the hand.

5. One should not touch his wet hand with the dry one. However, once one has dried his hands, he need not worry about touching one hand with the other. If someone else touches his hands while they are wet, he should dry his hands and wash again.

6. After washing, one should raise his hands so that the water from the part of his hands below his wrists (which is considered impure) should not fall on his hands (which are now purified). He recites the *Brocho* of "Al Netilas Yodayim" and dries his hands. He should avoid drying them on his clothing.

"Samuel said: 'For every ailment I have a remedy, except for the man who finishes a meal and does not walk at least four cubits (Amos) but goes immediately to sleep.'" (Baba Metzia 113)

"Wine in excess is injurious to health; in moderation, it is a benefit." (Derech Eretz 7)

"One should not be ill-tempered during a meal." (Kallah 10)

"Better a piece of dry bread in a contented home, than a potfull of meat in a quarrelsome home." (Proverbs 17)

"One should not be disturbed during a meal." (Kiddushin 45) (Orach Chayim 170)

"It is more worthy to house the wayfarer than to welcome G-d." (Shabbos 127)

BIRCHAS HAMAZON

The *Birchas Hamazon* consists of four *Brochos*. Originally there were only three. The fourth one of *Hatov V'Hameitiv* was added later. The *Brocho* of *Hazon* was composed by Moshe Rabeinu in gratitude fo the manna. The *Brocho* of *Nodeh* was composed by Yehoshua after entering

7. If one washed and was then unable to remember if he had said the *Brocho* of *"Al Netilas Yodayim"* he does not make the *Brocho*.

8. If someone forgot to make the *Brocho* before drying his hands, and he then remembers after he has already dried them, he says the *Brocho* of *"Al Netilas Yodayim"* if he has not yet made *"Ha'Motzee"*.

9. One is permitted to wash by immersing his hands in a stream or *Mikveh* holding at least 40 *Se'oh* (140 gallons) of water. However, if this is not possible and no cup is available, one still fulfills the *Mitzvah* of washing even if there is less than 40 *Se'oh* of water there. In the case of a natural spring or well, one doesn't need 40 *Se'oh*.

10. One can allow another person to pour the water onto his hands. This person may even be a youngster, or any individual not required to do *Mitzvos*. He may wash both of the other person's hands at once with the same cup.

12. One should wash as near as possible to the place where he will eat. If this is not possible, one should at least be able to see the food from where he is washing. If that, too, is difficult, one is still *yotzai*, regardless of where he washes.

13. During the meal, if one touched a part of his body which produces perspiration and is usually covered by clothing, or went to the bathroom to urinate he must wash again without a *Brocho*. In the case of defecation after having begun a meal, one should wash again with a *Brocho*. The above applies only if he intends to eat bread again.

14. If one does not have enough water to wash for both eating bread and going to a bathroom, he should wash and recite the *Brocho* of *"Al Netilas Yodayim,"* and then say *"Asher Yotzar."*

the Land of Israel. The *Brocho* of *Racheim* was composed by Dovid and Shlomo. The last *Brocho* of *Hatov V'Hameitiv* was composed by Rabban Gamliel the Elder in Yavneh after the victims at Betar were eventually buried.

"From the way a man pronounces his benedictions, we may tell whether he is a scholar or not." (Brochos 50)

"And you shall eat and be satisfied and you shall bless Hashem, your G-d, for the goodly land which He has given you." (Devorim 8:10)

This commandment to say *Birchas Hamazon* is found within a context that seems unrelated to the precept that the Jew bless G-d for his every meal. The chapter begins with an admonition that the people of Israel should remember their arduous travels in the desert and the land of G-d who protected and sustained them. There is prominent mention of the manna and its lesson. Israel is told that it will enter a goodly, prosperous land where food, water, and resources will be abundant. The nation is commanded to bless G-d for its plentiful, satisfy-

15. At a meal, some have the custom that the *Ba'al HaBayis* (host) wash last so he shouldn't have a long wait before he begins the meal, usually, however, the *Ba'al HaBayis* washes first.

III. THE UTENSIL (CUP):

1. If the cup leaks, it cannot be used for *Netilas Yodayim*. This remains true even if the cup can hold a *Reviyis* of water from the hole down. However, if the hole is used as a spout, and the cup holds a *Reviyis* from the hole down, the cup can be used. A cracked glass should not be used in any case, because it can easily break completely if hot water is poured into it. It is therefore not considered a utensil. A cup that cannot stand by itself holding a *reviyis* of water should not be used.

2. When repairing a hole in a utensil, one should use the same material that the rest of the utensil is made of.

3. If after washing and making *Ha'Motzee* one realizes that the utensil he used was not acceptable, he should wash again without a *Brocho*.

IV. THE WATER:

1. One should pour at least a *Reviyis* of water over his hands. If at all possible, he should pour a complete *Reviyis* of water over each hand.

2. Water which has become cloudy or discolored should not be used, unless the cloudiness is due to sand at the bottom of the cup.

3. The following types of water should not be used: water which has previously been used, water from which a snake or dog drank, water that is so hot that one would draw his hand away from it, and water not fit to be drunk by even a dog.

ing food and for the land that produced it. Then it is admonished not to forget G-d and His commandments, lest its prosperity blind it to the source of its blessing. Remember, it concludes, that G-d has given you the ability to accumulate your wealth, and that He has done it that you might serve Him better.

The custom is to remove all knives from the table before saying *Birchas Hamazon* because the table is compared to the sacrificial altar of the Temple concerning which it is written: "You shall not lift up any iron upon them" (*Devorim* 27:5). Iron shortens the life of man, while the altar helps prolong his days. It is, therefore, considered improper that iron, the element which shortens life should be raised on the "altar" which is intended to prolong life. (*Shulchan Aruch*)

Three men eating together, are duty bound under Jewish law to join together in reciting the Introduction to 'Grace After Meals'. We learn this from a scriptural text: '*Gadlu Lashem Itti, Unromemah Shemo Yachdav.*' ('Magnify the Lord with me, and let us exalt His name together.') (*Tehillim* 34:4)

"The imperative, *Gadlu* (magnify),

4. When washing by dipping one's hands into a stream, one says the *Brocho* of *"Al Netilas Yodayim."* If the water is unfit for *Netillah* but permissible for *Tevillah,* one says *"Al Tevillas Yodayim"* rather than *"Al Netilas Yodayim."*

5. Melted ice or snow can be used for washing. If the snow has not yet melted, one can immerse his hands into it if no other water is available. However, he must be able to dip his entire hand into it, and it must have 40 *Se'oh,* in one heap of snow.

6. If no water at all is available, one can wash with juice or milk, but not with wine.

7. One who is traveling on the road should go forward a distance of 2 ⅔ miles, or backward for a distance of approximately ¾ mile, to find water for *Netilas Yodayim.*

8. Where no water is available (such as in a desert), one may wrap his hands in a covering for the entire meal and then say *Ha'Motzee.*

LAWS OF THE MEAL

HAMOTZEE (The Blessing on Bread)

1. Before reciting the *Brocho* of *Hamotzee,* one should make a small cut with a knife in the *Challah* or bread, so he will know where to cut it later. The cut should not be so deep as to cause the *Challah* to break in half if it is picked up.

2. When reciting the words, *"lechem"* and *"min,"* the *mevoreich* (one who makes the blessing), should pause, in order to separate the sounds of the double *"mem".* One should hold the *challah* with all his fingers when saying the *Brocho,* and he should raise the *Challah* when saying

is written in the second plural. Hence it cannot be used when only one other person besides the one leading the *Benching* is present. It can be used only when the leader has more than one person at the table to address. Therefore, when less than three men have eaten at the table, the 'Introduction to Grace' cannot be recited." (*Brochos* 45a)

The reason why the blessing of "Blessed art Thou O Lord who in your compassion rebuilds Jerusalem, Amen" is the only *Brocho* in *Birchas Hamazon* ending with the word Amen,

is in order to make a distinction between the first three blessings which are based on Biblical law, and the fourth blessing, "Who is good and does good" which was instituted later on by Rabbinical authority.

The origin of the "Fourth Blessing" in the *Birchas Hamazon (Benching)* *"Hatov Vehameitiv"* "Who is good and does good" is explained in the following story:

The Fourth Blessing was instituted in memory of the thousands of Jews slain at Betar in the year 135 C.E. The town of Betar had five hundred

the name of *Hashem*. If one is reciting the *Brocho* on behalf of other individuals, he must have them in mind before starting the *Brocho*.

3. One is not allowed to talk after making the *Brocho* until he eats the *Challah*. The others included in the *Brocho* must wait until the *mevoreich* eats some of the bread before eating their own portion of bread. However, if anyone present has his own whole *Challah* before him, he may eat before the *mevoreich*.

4. There should be salt on the table, similar to the sacrifices on the *mizbeiach* (altar) in the *Beis Hamikdosh,* and one should dip the bread into the salt three times. If one forgot to place salt on the table, he need not go out of his way to get it.

5. If one said the *Brocho* of *She'Hakol* or *Borei Minei Mezonos* on the bread instead of *HaMotzee,* he should not make another *Brocho*.

6. Normally each one present says the *Brocho* of *HaMotzee* individually, since they don't eat together. However, on *Shabbos,* when *lechem mishneh* (two complete loaves of bread) is required, the *ba'al habayis* makes the *Brocho* for others, even if a *Talmid Chochom* is present. (The *ba'al habayis* may relinquish his right to the *Talmid Chochom* if he so wishes.)

7. If someone is washing before eating bread, and hears the *mevoreich* beginning to recite the *HaMotzee* over *lechem mishneh,* he should dry his hands quickly, be *yotzai* in the *HaMotzee,* and then recite the *Al Netilas Yodayim* before he eats the bread.

8. The *mevoreich* should begin eating his own piece of bread before dividing the remaining bread among the people at his table. He should place the pieces of bread before the people, but let them take the pieces

Jewish schools each of which had five hundred teachers. In addition, there were sixty thousand ordinary working people. During the reign of the Roman emperor Hadrian (132-35 C.E.), Betar, under the command of Bar Kochba was captured by Julius Severus, and all its inhabitants, both young and old, were put to death.

The Roman tyrant commanded that the dead should be left unburied. The bodies of the dead were piled high in a large vineyard outside the city limits and remained there throughout the last twenty-five years of Hadrian's life.

Miraculously, the bodies did not decompose. After the death of Hadrian, the bodies were buried in this same vineyard.

On the day that the dead of Betar could at last be given a proper burial, the Rabbis in Yavne ordained that the blessing "Who is good and causest good to happen" should henceforth be recited in the Grace after meals. "*Hatov*" ("Who is good") refers to the miraculous preservation of the bodies throughout the years passed and "*Vehameitiv*" ("Who does good") to the fact that, at last, the time had come

themselves. However, he should place a piece of bread directly in the hands of an *ovel* (mourner).

THE BREAD

1. If one plans to eat more than one piece of bread during the meal, he should first eat the *Challah* that is whole, unless he prefers the incomplete *Challah*. He should try to recite a *HaMotzee* over bread made with wheat before bread made with barley, over barley bread before rye, and over bread made with lighter flour before one with a darker color. One should recite the *HaMotzee* over the larger of two *Challahs* unless the smaller *Challah* is of a lighter flour.

2. Bread that is broken into small pieces (but the pieces are larger than a *Kezayis*) and cooked still requires a *Hamotzee*. If bread the size of a *Kezayis* has been soaked in soup or water, it also retains the *Brocho* of *Hamotzee*. If these pieces are smaller than a *Kezayis*, but still have the appearance and texture of bread, it is still a *Hamotzee*. Otherwise the *Brocho* of *Mezonos* is said. Such bread can regain the *Brocho* of *HaMotzee* according to most authorities if it is rebaked, without being sweetened, or filled with fruit, which would then classify it as cake. Thus, *Challah Kugel* may be *HaMotzee* or *Mezonos* depending on the manner in which it is prepared. Bread crumbs and matzoh meal require a *HaMotzee*.

3. There are three main categories of baked grain products requiring the Brocho of *Mezonos:* a) Cakes (dough heavily sweetened or kneaded with juice or oil instead of water, or heavily flavored in any other way); b) pies (filled with fruit, nuts, etc.) and crackers, and c) pretzels and pancakes.

when the bodies could be given a proper burial. *(Midrash Echa Rabthi,* Chapters 2 & 4; *Berachos* 48b; *Taanis* 31a; *Baba Basra* 121b)

"If one is meticulous in reciting the Birchas Hamazon *he may be certain that his livelihood will always be provided in a dignified manner."* (Mishna Brura 185, *Chapter which quotes Sefer Hachinuch)*

"Abraham accepted guests and after they ate and drank he then told them to make a blessing. They asked him, "What should we

bless?" *He told them to say, Blessed be the G-d of the world from whose food we ate."* (Medrash Rabba, Berashis *43)*

"He who doesn't say grace after meals transgresses the commandment, "Watch yourself; do not forget G-d your G-d." (Pesikta Dezutrasa.)

"You should recite the blessing after the meal with calmness, loudness and happiness of heart." (Sefer Charedim)

4. Bagels require a *Hamotzee* because they are baked after being cooked. Any cooked or fried grain product (non-baked) is a *Mezonos* and does not change its *Brocho* to *HaMotzee* even if used as a base for a meal (noodles, cereal, *kneidlach* and deep-fried doughnuts are common examples).

THE MEAL

1. If one says the *Brocho* of *HaMotzee* at the beginning of a meal, he need not make additional *Brochos* over most of the other foods eaten during the meal. However, wine drunk during the meal requires a separate *Brocho,* as do desserts such as fruits normally eaten at the end of the meal. If one eats a dessert as a side dish accompanying the meat, it needs no *Brocho;* however, if he eats the same item as a dessert at the end of the meal, he must make a *Brocho.* (In any case, a *Brocho Ach'ronah* need not be made on the dessert, since it is covered by *Birchas Hamazon.)* Most types of cakes or drinks consumed after the main courses of a meal, and fruits eaten as appetizers, do not require special *Brochos.* Whiskey drunk at the end of a meal needs a *She'hakol.* (Cakes fulfilling all three conditions cited above, need *Mezonos.)*

2. If one drinks wine before a meal, only for *Kiddush,* one need not make additional *Brochos* over wine drunk during the meal. Also, no *Brocho Ach'ronah* need be made on the wine, since it is covered by *Birchas Hamazon.*

3. One should eat some other food and drink something between fish and meat dishes eaten during a meal. One should use separate utensils for each, and should clean his hands between these courses.

4. If one falls asleep at a table, it is not considered a *hefsek* (interrup-

BLESSING HASHEM

"A man is obliged to utter a blessing on hearing evil tidings just as he does on hearing good tidings, as it is written, *'Uvchol Mo'adecho'* (and with all your might) teaching us that we are obliged to thank Him *'B'chol Midah Umidah'* (for whatever measure He metes out to us.)" (*Mishna Tractate Brochos* 9)

Reb Shmelke of Nikolsburg asked his Rebbe, Reb Dov Ber of Mezritch: "how is it possible to fulfill the injunction of our Sages, 'A man is obliged to utter a blessing on hearing evil tidings just as he does on hearing good tidings'"?

"Go along to the Beis Medrash," advised the Maggid of Mezritch, "and there you will find my disciple, Reb Zusya of Hanipoli. He will explain the *Mishnah* to you."

Throughout all his life, Reb Zusya lived in utter poverty. When he was told why Reb Shmelke had come to him, he said, "I am most surprised that our Rebbe should have sent you with this question to me, of all people. A

97

tion during the meal). However, he should still wash again without a *Brocho* before resuming the meal. Leaving the table to lie down and sleep for a while during a meal is considered an interruption. One must thereafter repeat the *Brochos of Al Netilas Yodayim* and *Hamotzee*.

5. If during the meal one is given wine to drink that is superior or equal to the wine upon which he made a *"Borei Pree HaGofen,"* he should say the *Brocho* of *"HaTov V'Hameitiv"* but need not say *"Borei Pree Hagofen"* again. This applies only if someone else drinks the wines along with him and if both bottles of wine are placed on the table for anyone to drink at will. In case there is one superior wine and one inferior wine on the table, to begin with, one should make the *"Borei Pree HaGofen"* on the superior wine. In this case, however, he loses the opportunity to say *"HaTov Ve'Hameitiv"* on the second wine.

6. There are many laws of health and etiquette applicable to the meal, including the following:

a) One should not speak while eating.

b) One should not eat too quickly.

c) If one is a guest at another's house, he should not refuse to eat a particular dish, though he does not have to complete the portion given to him.

d) One should not throw or otherwise abuse food.

e) One should not sleep right after a heavy meal.

f) One should not stare at another person while he is eating.

g) Bread or any other food should not be left lying on a floor or thrown into a ditch or any dirty place. However, it may be used as animal food for this is considered *L'Tzorech* (necessary).

7. If by accident a person drank mistakenly without saying a *Brocho*,

question like this should surely be put to a man who at some time has experienced something bad. I'm afraid that I can't be of any help to you since nothing evil has ever befallen me, even for a moment. Thank G-d, I have had only good things happening to me from the day I was born until today. So how could I know anything about evil?"

Reb Shmelke had his answer. This obligation to bless G-d on hearing evil tidings just as one does on hearing good tidings, was now clear. All a man

has to do is rejoice in his lot to the point that he does not consider anything a misfortune.

NACHUM ISH GAM-ZU

Many years ago in the time of the *Tanaim*, there lived a wise and good man in Israel named Nachum Ish Gam-Zu. Why was he called *Gam-zu*? Because whenever anything happened he always said, *"Gam zu le-tova*—this too is for the best." ("Whatever G-d does, He does for the best.")

It once happened that the Jewish people who lived in the land of Israel

he should swallow whatever is in his mouth and make a *Brocho* on the remaining drink if there is any. A *Brocho Ach'ronah* is always made (if required), regardless of whether or not a *Brocho Rishono* was made.

8. If a person accidentally ate without a *Brocho* and the food is still in his mouth, he should push the food to one side of his mouth and recite the proper *Brocho*. If he can take the food out of his mouth without ruining it, he should do so first and then recite the *Brocho*.

BIRCHAS HAMAZON (Grace After Meals)

1. One should recite *Birchas Hamazon* in the place where he ate. If before he washed, he intended to go elsewhere during the meal, then it is permissible to go somewhere else to continue the meal. In any case, if he already went somewhere else, he may continue his meal and say *Birchas Hamazon* in the second place. If he does not eat there, he should return to the place where he ate in order to say *Birchas Hamazon*.

2. If during the meal, one remembered that he had not yet davened, he should say *Birchas Hamazon* before going to *Shul* (or leaving the table to *daven*). If he went to *Shul* without saying *Birchas Hamazon*, a *Rav* should be consulted as to what to do.

3. One should leave some bread on the table before *Birchas Hamazon* so that if someone else comes, there will be some food to give him.

4. Pieces of bread larger than a kezayis shouldn't be thrown out. Even smaller pieces shouldn't be thrown where people walk.

5. All knives should be covered or removed from the table before *Birchas Hamazon* is said, except for *Shabbos*.

6. We have the custom to wash *Mayim Acharonim* before *Birchas*

---

said, "We shall send a gift to the king of the Romans, so that he will not make war on us."

And so they did. They took a box full of precious stones and pearls, a present for the Roman king. But who would carry the box to the king? Who would guard the precious stones on the long journey from the Land of Israel to Rome? The road was dangerous. There might be a storm at sea, or robbers might steal the box.

Where could they find an honest and trustworthy man to carry the exquisite gems to the king?

Then they thought of Nachum Ish

Gam-zu. "We will send our faithful Rabbi," they said.

Nachum agreed to take the box to the king, because he wanted to help his people. And so he started out on the distant and dangerous journey without fear. "This too, is for the best," he repeated to himself.

Nachum Ish Gam-Zu travelled on a ship for many days, and then he walked on foot all day until he reached an inn to rest in during the night.

Tired, Nachum said his prayers and lay down to sleep. He put the box with the valuable gift down beside him.

The innkeeper saw the strange box.

Hamazon. The water used should not be hot, and it should not be allowed to spill on the floor. One should wash *Mayim Acharonim* up to his knuckles. If there is no water available for this, one may use any liquid. Only one washing is needed, and *koach gavra* (pouring by a person) is not required. (i.e. the water may come from a tap). One should not eat after he has washed *Mayim Acharonim.*

7. Although there is no minimum requirement for a *Brocho Rishona,* one must eat at least a *Kezayis,* the size of an olive, before being able to say *Birchas Hamazon.*

8. One should concentrate completely while saying *Birchas Hamazon* and must not talk during this time. One should say *Birchas Hamazon* in Hebrew, if possible.

9. One answers *Omein* after his own *Brocho* of *Uvnei Yerushalayim,* in order to separate between the first three *Brochos,* which are from the Torah, and the fourth *Brocho* which was instituted by the *Rabbonim* of the *Mishnah.*

10. If someone is uncertain whether or not he has said *Birchas Hamazon,* he must repeat it, but if he was not satiated by the meal, he does not say *Birchas Hamazon.* If he cannot decide whether his meal was fully satisfying or not and he cannot remember whether he said *Birchas Hamazon* he should wash over and eat some more bread before saying *Birchas Hamazon.*

11. In the case of *Shabbos Rosh Chodesh, Retzei* is said before *Ya'ale V'Yovo* in *Birchas Hamazon,* because the former is said more frequently. However, if one reversed the order, he need not repeat *Birchas Hamazon.*

He was very curious to find out what was in it. So when Nachum Ish-Gam-Zu fell asleep, the innkeeper came over quietly and opened the box. The precious stones sparkled before him. The innkeeper's greed soon got the better of him, and he decided to act. He took out the pearls and the precious stones and he put dirt and pebbles in the box instead. Then he carefully closed the box and went to sleep.

Nachum Ish Gam-Zu woke up early the next morning. He said his morning prayers, took the box and went to the palace of the king. He had no inkling of what had happened the night before.

When he came before the king, Nachum said to him, "Greetings, your majesty. I have brought you a beautiful gift from the Jewish people of the Land of Israel."

The king saw the pretty box, and he, too, was very curious about its contents. With great anticipation, he opened it, and to his great consternation, found himself looking at nothing but dirt and a few small stones.

The king's face flushed with anger. "What is this?" he called out. "Do you call this a beautiful gift? Don't I have

12. If someone forgot to say Retzei on *Shabbos*, and he remembered before saying the *Brocho* of *Ha'Tov V'Hameitiv*, he should add a special Brocho there. (The *Brocho* is found in most *Siddurim*). However, if he remembered this after starting *Ha'Tov V'Hameitiv*, he must repeat the entire *Birchas Hamazon*. However, this does not apply to the meal of *Shalosh Seudos* where no such repetition is necessary.

13. Similarly, if one remembers having omitted *Ya'aleh V'Yovo*, he says a substitute *Brocho* before *Hatov Ve'Hameitiv*. If he already began *Ha'Tov Ve'Hameitiv*, on *Yom Tov* he must repeat the *Birchas Hamazon* as on *Shabbos*, but not on *Rosh Chodesh* or *Chol Hamoed*.

14. If someone forgot to say *Al Hanissim* on *Purim* or *Chanukah*, he may insert the prayer of *"HoRachamon Hu Ya'aseh Lonu Nissim V'Niflo'os K'moh She'asisah . . ."* after the *HoRachamon* prayers. However, even if he doesn't, he need not repeat the entire *Birchas Hamazon*.

15. If one extends his *Shalosh Seudos* meal into *Motzai Shabbos*, or if he realizes on *Motzai Shabbos* that he has not yet said *Birchas Hamazon* for the meal he ate on *Shabbos*, he should include *Retzai* in the *Birchas Hamazon*, provided that he has not yet davened *Ma'ariv*.

16. *Birchas Hamazon* should be recited while sitting. The *Brocho Ach'ronah* of *Al Hamichyo*, *Al Ho'etz* or *Al Hagefen* should preferably be said while sitting.

17. In order to *Bentch*, a person must eat bread in an amount the size of an egg or at least a *kezayis*. For a *Brocho Rishono*, however, there is no minimum amount. If a person had a full meal but never once during that meal did he eat a *kezayis* within the *Zman K'dai Achilas Pras*, within nine minutes, although the entire meal consisted of many *Kezaysim*, it is questionable if he should say *Birchas Hamazon* or not.

---

enough dirt and stones in my courtyard? I see that the Jews are making fun of me. I will punish them, and the man who brought the box will be put to death at once."

But Nachum Ish Gam-Zu was not at all afraid. As usual, he said, "This too is for the best. Whatever G-d does, He does for the best."

G-d saw that Nachum had trust in Him, and so He sent Eliyahu Hanovi to save him. Eliyahu disguised himself as one of the princes and came to the king.

"Why are you angry, your majesty?" he asked the king. "This is certainly not plain dirt. Why would the Jewish people do anything so foolish as to anger you? Maybe this is special dirt. Let us try to throw a little of it into the air. Perhaps it will turn into swords and arrows and we will be able to overcome the enemies of the king, just as it happened to Abraham, the father of the Jewish people."

The king thought for a minute and said, "Good idea. Let us try." So they threw a little of the dirt into the air, and

18. One should not delay reciting *Birchas Hamazon* long after the meal is over. If one did delay *Bentching,* as long as he feels satiated from the meal he may still say *Birchas Hamazon.* This may be as long as 2-3 hours after a full meal. In case of a snack, he may not make a *Brocho Ach'ronah* after 72 minutes.

19. A person who is drunk and cannot speak clearly, should nevertheless *Bentch.*

LAWS OF MEZUMAN

1. When three or more males over thirteen eat a meal together, they must say *Birchas Hamazon* as a group, with one of them conducting the *Bentching* and the others responding. This is called a *Zimun.* The group is called a *Mezuman.*

2. The leader begins by calling for the group to *"Bentch."* This is said in any language *("Rabosai Nevoreich," "Lomir Bentschen," "Gentlemen,"* etc.) The others respond with a *Posuk* of praise to *Hashem ("Yehi Shem")* repeated by the leader. Then the actual *Zimun* begins. The leader says, *"Birshus Moronon . . ."* (by your permission . . .) *"Nevoraich She'Ochalnu Mishelo".* (When ten or more men are present, the name of *Hashem* is inserted into the *Zimun: "Nevoreich 'Elokeinu' She'Ochalnu Mishelo."* At the mention of G-d's name, one rises slightly.) The others respond *"Boruch She'Ochalnu Mishelo"* etc. and the leader responds in the same way as found in all *Siddurim.*

3. Those that ate as a group must *Bentch* with *Mezumon.* Those that happened to be eating at the same time but were not joined as a group (such as in a restaurant, or school lunchroom) may *Bentch Bimezumon.*

instantly the dirt turned into swords and arrows. And with these weapons the king would conquer all his enemies.

The king was overjoyed. He called Nachum Ish Gam-Zu before him and said, "Please forgive me for being angry at you. You have brought me a very worthy gift indeed. I have, therefore, decided to refill the box with gold and pearls instead of the wondrous soil that you have brought me. And please thank the Jewish people for me.

Nachum smiled. "I always said that everything is for the best," he said.

And so he took the box filled with precious stones and returned happily to the Land of Israel. (*Taanis* 21a)

There was once a man who was both very wealthy and very proud. He used to say, "Money is the best proof of wisdom."

Once a plague broke out among his cattle and all his oxen died. He did not have a single one left with which to plow his numerous large fields. (This occurred many years before the invention of tractors and farm machinery.) The land became overgrown with weeds, and it was ruined.

What did the man do? He took a

In any case, if three or more sitting at one table have all ended their meal together, they must Bentch *Bimezumon*, that is, no one may Bentch individually.

4. It is not necessary for all three participants to actually eat for the same duration for *Zimun* to take place. As long as one is sitting by the table and still has an appetite to eat his favorite dessert, he is considered as still-eating, and others may begin eating with him and join as a *Mezumon*.

5. If two ate bread, a third can join the *Mezumon*, regardless of the type of food he ate, as long it was not merely water. If he is able and willing to eat cake, he should do so. (It is preferable that one wash and make a *Motzee* in order to join as a third member in a *Mezumon*, but custom follows the first approach.)

6. In case of a *Mezumon* of ten, seven must have eaten bread. The others join as long as they ate or drank anything, except water.

7. It is a *Mitzvah* to arrange to Bentch with a *Mezumon*. Therefore, two who ate should try to invite a third to join them, and a larger group should try to get others to complete the required ten so they can add the word *"Elokeinu."*

---

purse filled with 100 gold coins and set out for a distant village to buy oxen with which to plow his fields.

On the way, he met Eliyahu Hanavi, dressed as a poor old man, who asked him where he was going.

"I'm off to a certain village to buy oxen."

"You should say, '*Im Yirtzeh Ha-shem*,' ('If G-d is willing')," remarked Eliyahu Hanavi.

"Well, whether G-d is willing or not—I have plenty of money in my purse to do as I please," he replied, and he set off on his journey.

On the way, his purse fell out of his pocket without his noticing it. When he reached the village and had picked out the oxen he wished to buy, he found to his dismay that he did not have his purse with which to pay for them.

He returned home and took some

more money from his plentiful supply. He set off on a different route in order not to meet that old man. This time he met Eliyahu disguised as a different old man, who asked him:

"My son, where are you going?"

"To purchase some oxen," he replied.

"You should say, 'G-d willing,'" the old man rebuked him.

"What's G-d got to do with it? I've got money in my purse to do as I please."

The man continued on his way, and when he felt drowsy, he lay down to sleep in a field. Eliyahu came along and sneaked his purse out of his pocket. As had happened the first time, the man had to return home empty-handed to get a fresh supply of gold coins.

He set out once again for that distant village, this time on his original

8. If two men have ended their meal and wish to *Bentch*, the third party must interrupt his meal to answer to their *mezumon*. He may not continue his meal until after the *mevorach* (leader) finishes the first *Brocho* of *Birchas Hamazon*. *(Hazon es Hakol)*.

9. Two may interrupt their meal to join a third individual who wishes to *Bentch Be'mezumon*, but they are not required to do so.

10. One who interrupted his meal to answer to a *Mezumon* is no longer obligated to *Bentch Bemezumon*. He may eat further and join two others who are not in another *Mezumon*.

11. Two groups of people eating in the same room but at different tables, may join for a *Mezumon* provided they are able to see each other.

12. A group of ten should not separate into smaller groups, thus losing their chance to say *"Elokeinu,"* just as a group of three should not separate and *Bentch* individually.

13. If there is a large party in a dining room or hall, and three of those present must leave early, they should join quietly for a *mezuman*. If one must leave early, he should have this in mind to begin with.

14. Men who have eaten a meat meal may join in a *mezuman* with someone else who has eaten dairy. In this case, it is best that the one who has eaten dairy be the *mevoreich*.

15. The *mevoreich* should be someone who has eaten at least one piece of bread the size of an egg and is satiated from it. It is best that one who is still thirsty should not be the *mevoreich*.

16. It is appropriate that a guest be the *mevoreich*, and he should not refuse the honor. This is especially true if the guest is a *Kohein* or a *Talmid Chochom*.

---

route. Once again, he met the old man who asked where he was going.

"To buy oxen, G-d willing," the man replied.

"Peace be with you and may you prosper," answered the old man.

At that moment, without knowing it, Eliyahu replaced all the lost coins in the man's purse. When the man arrived in the village to buy the oxen, he was upset that he could not buy all the beautiful cattle he saw, since he had insufficient money with him.

He opened his purse to pay for two oxen and to his great surprise and pleasure, found his purse filled with the 200 gold coins that he previously lost. Now he was able to buy all that he wanted. It turned out to be an excellent year, and the harvest brought in far more than he had dared to hope for.

That man learned his lesson, as we all should—*Hashem's* blessings are bestowed because of His loving kindness to us. We, in turn, have to acknowledge this *"Chessed"* by remembering to recite *"Brochos"* before eating *Hashem's* food.

"Im Yirtzeh Hashem" (If G-d is will-

17. The custom today is to say *Birchas Hamazon,* over a cup of wine on *Shabbos* or festive occasions.

The *Mevoreich* should hold the cup of wine in his stronger hand and lift it a *tefach* (at least three inches). The *Brocho* on wine must be said at the end, and a full *reviyis* must be drunk by him to avoid the problem of a *Brocho Ach'ronah.*

ing) should always be in our minds and hearts, and on our lips, for all that happens is His Will.

"Our table is compared to that of the altar in the Temple. We should therefore behave with due reverence when at the table, just as if we were worshipping before the altar of G-d." (Chagiga 27)

כשרות
Kashrus

INTRODUCTION—KASHRUS

"Sanctify yourself and be you holy; for I am holy" (Vayikra 11:44).

"You shall be holy unto Me for I the L-rd am holy and I have set you apart from other peoples to be Mine" (Vayikra 20:26).

This is the rationale of the laws of Kashrus.

1. The Torah specifically states which animals and fowl are permitted to be eaten and which are not. In the case of animals, the permitted ones are listed, and in the case of birds, those that are forbidden are listed. The signs which differentiate kosher animals from non-kosher ones are given explicitly: the kosher animals have cloven hoofs and chew their cud. It has been verified that every animal whose hoofs are cloven, chews the cud, with the exception of the pig, as indicated by the Torah.

2. The prohibited birds are few in number, and total only 24 species. The oral tradition of the Torah has made clear to distinguish the kosher from the non-kosher. First, all birds of prey are forbidden. All birds that have the characteristic of picking food right out of the air without waiting for the food to reach the ground are prohibited. Once it has been established that a bird does not prey, it becomes necessary to examine it further. There is considerable difficulty in ascertaining whether an unknown bird is kosher. Therefore we can only eat those fowl which tradition has already accepted as being kosher.

KASHRUS
INTRODUCTION

Among the different classifications of laws in the Torah are the *Chukim*. These are commandments whose rationales are somewhat unclear to us, such as *Kashrus*. Because the reasons for these *Mitzvos* are not specifically stated, there have been some Jews throughout the ages who have considered these laws irrelevant and have refused to obey them. However, they have forgotten that these laws come directly from *Hashem*, as do all other laws, and He, of course, knows the full reason for all His commandments. Therefore, our ignorance of His purpose should not lead us to believe that these *Mitzvos* are unimportant. It is only our lack of perspective that prevents us from fully understanding them.

3. The marks by which clean fish may be recognized are explicitly written in the Torah. All that have fins and scales are kosher. It has been verified that all fish which have scales have fins; but the reverse is not true: many fish have fins and no scales.

Insects, creeping things, and the like are abominations and are prohibited as food.

4. Animals and fowl which have died of themselves are called *Nevela* and are forbidden to be eaten. Kosher species may not be used unless properly slaughtered. A limb torn from a living animal is prohibited. An animal on the verge of death cannot be made fit to eat by slaughtering it in the prescribed manner. An animal that is suffering from one of the 18 categories of affliction, from which it will surely die, is considered a *Trefah* and it may not be eaten even when it is ritually slaughtered. Scripture itself designates an animal torn by another animal as *Trefah* and unfit for food, and the Oral Law explains the prohibition to include a wide variety of afflictions.

5. The Torah states: "You shall slaughter as I have commanded you" (*Devorim* 12). The proper method of slaughtering an animal is to sever its esophagus and trachea; of slaughtering a fowl, to sever at least one of these. The cut must be made with a proper slaughter knife. Only an observant Jew may be entrusted with the work. It is customary for men and not women to do the slaughtering. The slaughterer must not only review the laws carefully on a regular basis, but must maintain a certain moral standard as well.

6. A person who becomes a slaughterer must not only be conversant with the laws of *Shechita,* but must also not be of a nervous disposition, lest that lead to imperfect slaughtering.

7. In the laws of ritual slaughter, there are five things to avoid in making the *Shechita* cut. The things to be avoided are: hesitation, undue pressure, burrowing, cutting outside the specified zone, and lacerations. The incision must be made without hesitation, ensuring great swiftness,

This is comparable to a man observing a painting in a museum. He notices crowds gathering in front of the painting, admiring its beauty and design. However, to the man, the painting appears to be just a series of dark and ugly splotches, and he cannot understand the painting's popularity. He complains aloud that the painting makes no sense at all. But then someone notices that he is looking at the painting through smeared up darkened glasses, and that this is altering his view of it.

Similarly, if we do not always appreciate the beauty of the Torah's logic, it does not mean that the beauty does not exist, but only that our ability to see it has been clouded.

Throughout the years, there have

when the unusual sharpness of the blade is taken into consideration. By the time the cut is completed, the animal is no longer conscious. Before a knife is used for killing, it must be examined along the blade and along both edges. If the slightest dent is observed, the knife is not used. The examination must be made with the utmost concentration, as small imperfections are difficult to detect. To avoid the possibility of undue pressure, the knife may not be too short; it should be at least twice as long as the diameter of the neck of the animal to be slaughtered.

8. After a fowl or a beast is killed, its blood is covered with earth, or something similar to it. Blood of cattle is not covered: neither is the blood of any wild animal or bird improperly slaughtered. Both before killing and before covering the blood, *Brochos* are recited, praising the L-rd who has given us these sanctifying laws.

9. After *Shechita,* the forbidden fat, known as *Chelev,* must be removed. Chelev can physically be distinguished from ordinary fat by the way in which it adheres loosely to the flesh and can be readily peeled off, while ordinary fat is more firmly attached. *Chelev* is prohibited only in oxen, sheep and goats; *chelev* of any other species is permissible from a Kosher animal.

10. After the animal is trimmed of fat there still remains the *Gid Hanasheh* (sinew of Jacob/sciatic nerve) which must be excised. There are two sinews: the inner one, near the bone; the outer one, near the flesh. They, together with their connecting tissues must be cut out.

11. The last thing to be removed is the blood. The Torah mentions many times its prohibitions that no blood whatsoever should be eaten. The first step towards the removal of the blood is the excision of a number of larger veins. The meat is then salted.

12. Before the meat is salted, it should be thoroughly washed and soaked in water for about a half hour. If the soaked meat is cut prior to salting, it must be resoaked. Soaking too long should be avoided, for

been many reasons offered for the laws of *Kashrus.* Some have asserted that the laws of *Kashrus* were only a temporary health measure. For instance, they say that pork was prohibited so that Jews would not suffer from trichinosis, and that the laws of salting meat were a way of preserving the meat before refrigeration was discovered. Thus, they claim, these laws of *Kashrus* are no longer necessary.

However, this approach is wrong. While it is certainly true that the Torah is concerned about people's health and well-being this is not the only rationale for *Kashrus.* The Torah is also concerned with our spiritual well-being and with our inner purity. Therefore, when the Torah tells us to avoid certain foods, it thereby provides for our spiritual cleanliness. Foods which are inherently unclean and disgusting,

meat soaked twenty four hours is considered as having been pickled with its blood and becomes prohibited. It is customary to set aside a special vessel for the soaking of meat, and that pail is used for no other purpose. Meat should be soaked not later than three days after its slaughter. Neither very fine nor very coarse salt should be used. Every side of the meat should be salted, and fowls must be covered with salt inside and outside. Meat should be salted in a vessel with a perforated bottom. Care should be taken not to salt meat in a closed vessel, for the pieces immersed in the bloody salt water which gathers at the bottom may not be eaten. Meat should not be cut during the process of salting. If it was cut, the meat must again be immediately washed and salted. The length of the salting process is approximately an hour and then the salt is washed off. It should be rinsed off three times. Care should be taken not to cook the meat without first washing off the salt, for if it is so cooked, both the pot and its contents are rendered *Trefah*. If a mistake was made, a *Rav* should be consulted.

There are special laws for removing blood from liver (since it has different properties). The liver cannot be simply salted, but must be broiled.

MILK AND MEAT

The *Posuk*, "Lo Sivashel G'dee B'Chalev Imo" *is mentioned three times in the Torah, and teaches us that one is not allowed to:*

a) cook, fry, or roast milk and meat together;

b) eat milk and meat which were cooked together;

c) derive any pleasure or benefit from this mixture (i.e., one cannot sell it or give it as a present to a gentile, or even feed it to one's dog.)

These things are "Osser Min HaTorah" *(Biblical prohibitions).*

1. By Rabbinic decree, chicken and other fowl were given the legal status of meat with respect to the laws of 'milk and meat.' Therefore, the

such as the meat of animals that died of disease, or the products of insects and the unsanitary pig, are not kosher, and those who eat them have little regard for their own purity. Similarly, foods of naturally vicious animals, such as birds of prey and beasts of the forest, are prohibited, while products of domesticated animals, like the chicken and the cow, are allowed. We are, in a way, influenced by what we eat. Therefore, we must base our actions on the peaceful ways of the animals that are permitted to be eaten. *(Ramban, Parshas Shemini* and *Parshas R'eh).*

Because of this, we must be very careful of the food that we allow to enter our bodies. We must make sure that the foodstuffs we buy do not contain any non-kosher ingredients. We should ascertain that the meat we buy

prohibition of eating, listed above applies to fowl as well as to meat. The Rabbis also prohibited the eating of meat and milk products together even if they were not cooked together.

2. A difference between what is "Ossur Min HaTorah" and "Ossur Me'D'Rabbonon" is that one may derive benefit from, although not eat, foods prohibited by the Rabbonim.

3. The Issur (prohibition) of "Bosor B'Cholov" (meat in milk) does not apply to milk cooked with meat from a non-kosher animal (e.g., pork, horse). Consequently, one is allowed to feed dog-food from a non-kosher animal, that contains milk products to a dog.

4. One may eat eggs with milk even though they came from hens (birds) which are Fleishig (meat product). However, if an egg is found in a slaughtered chicken, even though it may be a fully developed egg (with a shell), it is best not to cook it together with milk. If it is not a fully developed egg, then it's considered part of the chicken.

5. Dishes, pots or any kind of utensils that were used for milk or milk products should not be used for meat, and vice versa. If pots and pans normally used for meat dishes are mistakenly used for hot dairy foods (or vice versa), then the food cooked or fried in them is forbidden, if the pot has been used within the previous 24 hours (Ben Yoma), and the utensil cannot be used until it has been kashered. (Consult your Rabbi for this procedure.) Not all utensils can be kashered after becoming treif (non-kosher), e.g. chinaware.

6. Every Jewish household must have two sets of tableware and kitchenware, one set for milk products and the other set for meat products. (A few utensils should be kept separately for use as Pareve, which means neither milk nor meat.)

7. Soap, steel wool or dish brushes used to wash one set of dishes should not be used for the other. One should also have separate dish pans and sink grates. If one has only one sink, one should wash dishes either on separate Milchig (pertaining to milk) or Fleishig (pertaining to

was properly prepared. We cannot take anything for granted in this respect, and we should not rely solely upon our own judgment. We should be as careful of not eating non-kosher foods as we are of not eating poison.

THE KOSHER REWARD

It was in the early 1900's. Moshe was a young man who lived in a Jewish ghetto in Russia. It was a very poor town and Moshe didn't own very much. However, he did have one tremendous treasure which compensated for everything else he lacked. Moshe possessed a tremendous amount of Emunah, faith in Hashem. Although times were very hard for the Jews of Russia, Moshe didn't worry.

meat) sink grates, or in separate dish pans, but not directly in the sink.

8. If one has just eaten a milk meal or a Milchig snack, likc a milchig candy bar or ice cream, he should make sure to wash his hands and rinse and clean his mouth to remove any traces of the milk before proceeding to eat meat. The cleaning is done by brushing the teeth and rinsing thoroughly or by eating a food such as a piece of bread, cake, or apple and then drinking water.

9. The only time this doesn't apply is after eating hard cheese that has been aged over 180 days (e.g. certain imported Swiss cheeses). In this case one must wait six hours before eating meat. After eating any other cheeses, one does not have to wait a prescribed amount of time before eating meat.

10. After eating meat or meat products, one must wait six hours (according to most customs) before eating dairy products (and in this respect, everyone should follow the custom of his parents.) If after waiting the proper amount of time, one finds that he still has particles of meat stuck between his teeth, he should clean his teeth thoroughly and rinse out his mouth, but he is not obligated to wait any longer before eating dairy.

11. One is permitted to eat milk foods immediately after eating Pareve foods cooked in a Fleishig pot or in an oven which is usually used for meat. For example, after eating a piece of potato kugel cooked in a Fleishig pot, one may drink milk or eat a Milchig food. However, one should not eat the two together.

12. One must have separate tablecloths for meat and for dairy foods. If one is eating Milchig foods and someone else wants to eat meat, there must either be a divider between the two of them or separate place-mats. If not, they should not eat these together at the same table. Also, left-over bread, challah or vegetables, left-over from a Fleishig meal, should not be used with a subsequent Milchig meal and vice versa.

13. If a drop of milk falls on the outside of a pot containing boiling meat,

He knew that just as a father cares for his children, Hashem was watching over him and his neighbors.

One day, a message arrived from the Russian government informing Moshe that he was being drafted into the army. He was to report to the induction center the following week. Moshe sat in a daze, staring at the message before him. He had been able to cope with almost anything during his life, but this?

"What shall I do?" he wondered to himself. "I can't enter the army. Everyone knows that the Jews in the Russian army are forced to eat non-kosher foods. Never in my life have I eaten anything non-kosher, and now I

or similarly, if meat sauce or gravy falls on the outside of a pot of boiling milk, a Rabbi should be consulted, since hot liquid penetrates the sides of the pot. If the drop of liquid or food actually falls into the pot, one should be sure to ask a competent Rabbi whether it is permissible to eat the cooked food, or to use that pot again before *kashering* it. It will depend, in part, on the proportion of the drop that fell into the pot to the amount of food that actually was in the pot, therefore, one should note the amounts of milk and meat therein.

14. If a *Milchig* spoon or fork was accidentally put into a hot *Fleishig* food, or vice versa, or if the wrong lid was put on the pot, a competent Rabbi must be consulted as to the usability of both the food and the utensil. If one fails to do anything about that utensil and continues to use it, it jeopardizes the *Kashrus* of subsequent foods used with that utensil. This applies only to hot foods. If the food was cold, and the spoon was cold and wiped clean, then one has to merely wash off the spoon.

15. If a *Fleishig* fork or knife was put into a cold *Milchig* product, or if a *Milchig* fork or knife was put into a cold *Fleishig* product, one must consult a competent Rabbi as to what is done with the knife or fork and food, as long as the fork or knife is completely clean.

If one used a cold *Fleishig* knife to slice a *Pareve* food (for instance bread) to be used with a dairy food, that bread may be used with a *Milchig* meal, provided of course, that the knife was totally clean and did not have any meat particles on it.

16. Bread should not be made with milk because one may forget that it is *Milchig* and eat it with a meat meal. The only time it may be made with milk is if it is molded into a distinctive shape so that everyone knows just by looking at it that it was made with milk.

PAS AKUM (Bread Baked by a Gentile)

1. Our Sages made a *g'zairoh* (decree) prohibiting us from eating a gentile's home-made bread *(pas akum)* or cake made by a gentile from

am going to be forced to eat non-kosher foods day after day! I must try everything possible to have this order cancelled. But what can I do? No Jew is powerful enough to get himself excused from serving as a soldier."

Moshe decided that there was only one thing left for him to do—that which Jews have done all through the ages in times of distress. He diverted his thoughts from his awesome problem and spent his days fasting and praying to *Hashem.* "Please, *Hashem,*" he would pray, "You know that I would never willfully eat non-kosher foods or disobey any of the other laws of the Torah. Please don't put me into a situation where the Russians will force me to transgress Your *Mitzvos.*"

the five species of grain (wheat, barley, rye, oats and spelt) even if the ingredients are Kosher. The reason for this is that the Sages wanted to prevent the Jews from socializing with and assimilating into the other nations. Many Jews are careful about not buying even commercially-made gentile bread, which has supervised kosher ingredients, if Jewish-made bread is available. If a Jew helps in the baking process, even if only increasing the heat or putting the bread into the furnace, it removes the prohibition of *pas akum.*

BISHUL AKUM (Cooked Food by a Gentile)

1. Our Sages also prohibited eating food cooked by a non-Jew *(bishul akum).* This applies to foods that are served at a banquet *(Oleh Al Shulchan Melochim),* like meat and chicken, and to those foods which are not usually eaten raw. For example, there is no *g'zairoh* on a baked apple. Because of these two exemptions, many foods will not fall into the category of *bishul akum.* Candies, coffee and tea are not considered important enough to go under the prohibition of *bishul akum.* However, strict supervision must still be maintained as to the *Kashrus* of the product.

2. If a Jew helps kindle the fire or helps with the cooking of the food until it is 1/3 done, the *issur* of *bishul akum* is removed, even if the gentile then removes the pot and puts it back on the stove to cook later. If a gentile started cooking the food and it was more than 1/3 done, then the food is permissible if the further cooking can still improve the dish and it is done by a Jew.

3. If the cooked dish is a mixture of foods, some of which are edible raw and some of which aren't, it is only prohibited when the main part is not edible raw, like a meat casserole with vegetables. This prohibition does not apply to foods that are salted, preserved or smoked by a gentile.

4. If it happens that the gentile cooked the food completely and it is definitely *bishul akum,* then not only is the food prohibited but many

Then came the night before Moshe was to be inducted into the Russian army. He tossed and turned until he finally fell asleep.

"Moshe!" said a familiar figure in the dream.

"Father! How good to see you. I need your help."

"I know what the problem is, Moshe. There is nothing to worry about, To-morrow, when you go down for your induction, the doctor will ask you if you have any physical disabilities. When he does this, simply point to your chest."

"But I can't do that! I know that I am physically fit. When the doctor sees that I lied, I'll be severely punished."

"I told you, my son. Don't worry! Just have faith as you always do."

authorities hold that the pot must also be *kashered*. One must be especially careful to avoid this prohibition when one has a gentile maid who helps with the cooking.

CHOLOV AKUM (Dairy Foods from a Gentile)

1. Milk that comes from a farm owned by a non-Jew is prohibited because the milk may be mixed with the milk from a non-kosher animal. However, if a Jew does the milking or supervises the milking, then it is permissible. Also, if it is being done on a Jew's farm where it is known that the Jew can walk in at any time and observe the milking, then it is permissible. Many Jews today use non-Jewish milk because they rely on government regulations concerning milk. (Decision of Rav Moshe Feinstein, *Shlita*)

2. Cheese is *ossur* (prohibited) unless the actual cheese-making process is supervised by a Jew. Butter made by a gentile from non-Jewish milk is permissible (since the churning of butter can only be done with milk from a kosher animal and not with milk from a non-kosher animal). A Jew may not, however, make butter out of milk that comes under the *g'zairoh* of *cholov akum* (milk from a non-Jew) since the *issur* cannot be removed from the milk by making it into butter. (Some say that the laws of butter apply to cream as well.)

3. Some are of the opinion that *cholov akum* does not apply to powdered milk.

KOSHER PRODUCTS

1. If the manufacturer or supplier of kosher foods also produces non-kosher products, the question arises whether the same machinery was used in the production of both the kosher and non-kosher items. If so, the products might not be kosher.

2. By law, some products don't have to list all of their ingredients, some of which may be of non-kosher origin. Therefore, relying on a listing of ingredients to certify *kashrus,* is not correct.

Moshe awoke. Did his dream mean something? Was this *Hashem*'s way of sending help? He would find out soon enough. . . .

It was Moshe's turn.

"Well, young man, you look fit enough to me. Any physical disabilities?"

Moshe said nothing. He merely pointed to his chest.

The doctor looked at Moshe suspiciously. He pulled out his stethoscope and listened to Moshe's chest. After a few moments, he looked up at Moshe and said, "Sorry, young man. You're not physically fit to serve in the army."

Moshe walked out of the induction center, with tears in his eyes and in a

3. A company may produce some items under Rabbinic Supervision, yet not all of their products will have *Kashrus* certification. Those without *Hashgacha* should not be used.

4. Most of the foods we buy need Rabbinic Supervision *(hashgacha)* to make sure that their ingredients and their preparation have conformed with the laws of *Kashrus.*

Buying Kosher foods today really presents no problem. One merely has to look for the different symbols which assure us of the *Kashrus* of the products. The letter K found on some foods indicates that the company has Rabbinic Supervision, but in this case it is important to ascertain who the rabbinic supervisor is. One should not rely on past experience, but should look for the *Kashrus* seal each time that one buys a prod·ict.

Besides checking for the *Kashrus* seal, one should also look for an indication as to whether the product is *Pareve* or *Milchig.* Only those products that say *Pareve* can be assumed to be *Pareve.* Those products bearing just the *Hashgacha* may be dairy even though no dairy ingredients are listed, since they might have been prepared with dairy equipment which makes them *pareve* but necessitates their not being eaten together with meat.

WHAT QUESTIONS OF KASHRUS ARE WE CONCERNED ABOUT IN THE PREPARATION OF FOODS?

1. The main problem in the manufacture of cakes, cookies, crackers, cake mixes and dry cereals is the use of shortening, gelatin, oils, emulsifiers, mono and diglycerides, and margarine of non-kosher or animal origin. It is possible for any cake or pastry product to contain non-kosher glycerides even if the ingredient label indicates vegetable shortening. For this reason one must always look for an indication of *hashgacha* before purchasing these products.

2. Many of the dry cereals contain *Milchig* ingredients which, of

---

hushed voice so that no one could hear, he said, *"Baruch She'asa Lee Nais B'Makom Hazeh."* (Blessed be He who performed a miracle for me in this place.)

BLIND TRUST

A *Godol* was once in a distant land where people didn't recognize him. A simple Jew, upon seeing the distinguished looking Rabbi, thought he

might be a *shochet* (ritual slaughterer) and asked him to slaughter a chicken for him. The rabbi declined, explaining he was not a licensed *shochet.*

"Could you lend me $1,000?" asked the Rabbi.

"If I don't know you, how can I be sure that you will repay me?" was the reply.

"Since you don't know me, how

course, can not be eaten with meat products. One should, therefore, check the ingredients first.

3. A cream substitute which is classified as non-dairy, is not automatically non-Milchig. It may contain sodium casinate, a milk derivative, which need not be listed as a dairy product. However, according to the laws of *Kashrus*, it is still considered *Milchig*. One should, therefore, use only cream substitutes with Rabbinic supervision.

4. Gelatin and rennet, which are used in the preparation of desserts, puddings, and some candies, are of animal origin. Most prominent halachic authorities prohibit the use of gelatin made from animals that have not been slaughtered and prepared in accordance with the laws of *Kashrus*. There is a very limited supply of Kosher gelatin on the market and it is generally not available for desserts and puddings. Some candies under strict Rabbinic Supervision may contain gelatin with proper Rabbinic approval. Most marshmallows contain gelatin of animal origin (non-kosher source).

5. French fried potatoes must have Rabbinic Supervision because they are fried in oil, which may be of non-kosher origin. And non-kosher utensils may have been used in their preparation.

6. Frostings used on cakes, pastries and other similar desserts must have Rabbinic supervision because they almost always contain mono or di-glycerides, shortening, or gelatin, all of which may be of non-kosher origin. The same pertains to whipped cream and toppings. The so-called non-dairy whipped creams usually contain ingredients which are halachically *milchig*.

7. Ice Cream, Ices and Sherbets:

a) Ice cream and sherbets may contain stabilizers, emulsifiers, gelatin, mono or di-glycerides or polysorbate 65 and 80, all of which may be of non-kosher origin.

b) Ices may possibly contain gelatin and tartaric acid of non-kosher origin.

could you rely upon me to slaughter the chicken according to *halacha* (Jewish law)?" asked the guest.

"*You should choose a shochet who has fear of sin, since most people need this Mitzvah in order to eat, and there are a lot of intricate laws that must be carried out. If you have a shochet who has fear of sin, he will carry out all the laws of She-* chita. *If he has not, you might eat treif.*" (Sha'arei Teshuva Le Rabbenu Yonah).

THE HONEST PICTURE

A man entered a kosher butcher store, and asked the owner for references of his reliability on *Kashrus*.

"How can you doubt my credentials?" asked the butcher. "Don't you see how religious I am? Why, I even

c) Sherbet by definition contains milk and milk products. According to federal standards, it must contain a minimum of 2% butterfat and 2-5% of total milk solids.

Children should be aware of the fact that most of the truck vending ice cream concerns do not have Kosher certification. Only those ice creams, ices and sherbets which have reliable Rabbinic supervision should be used.

8. Most juices, canned or frozen, don't need Rabbinic supervision. However, grape juice and also grape soda have similar halachic considerations as wine and are prohibited without *hashgacha*.

9. Macaroni, noodles and spaghetti should have *Hashgacha* because they might contain glycerol monostearate, which may be of animal origin.

10. A product labeled as vegetable oil or vegetable shortening is NOT guaranteed to be Kosher. Rabbinic supervision is still needed to ascertain that it is of Kosher origin and that it has not come in contact with any animal oil or shortening.

11. The above also applies to potato chips, corn chips, pop corn and pretzels, which must have Rabbinic supervision, to determine whether the oils used in cooking and frying are of a Kosher source and whether the utensils used are Kosher. Even if there is *hashgacha,* one should still check the ingredients to make certain that the product isn't *Milchig.* (For instance, pop corn or pretzels may be prepared with butter.)

12. The chief problem with candy and confectionary items is that they may contain ingredients of non-kosher origin, and the machinery and utensils used in their production may be *treif.* The following are some of the questionable ingredients usually found in candy: gelatin, mono or di-glycerides, emulsifiers, stabilizers, glycerine, monostereates, stearic acid, fat preservatives, polysorbate 60 and vegetable oil.

13. Most chewing gums contain glycerine and/or glycerol, and monos-

keep pictures of famous rabbis in my shop window!"

The man replied, "If your picture would be hanging in the window, and the famous rabbi would be standing behind the counter, then I would definitely buy the meat. However, the reverse situation is not a proof of *Kashrus!*"

A wealthy Jew from Pest, who did not observe the *Shabbos* and the festivals, and who ate non-kosher food, happened to be present at a Chassidic gathering presided over by Reb Chaim of Sanz. According to the custom at the *'tish'* (table) in certain Chassidic circles, the Rebbe partook of the food which was served to him, and then offered the remaining portion (*sh'rayim*) to his disciples, each of whom tasted a morsel. Reb Chaim offered a little of the food to this individual too—

tearate and need Rabbinic supervision. These ingredients are not found listed on the gum wrapper, but are contained within the ingredient listing of gum base or softeners.

14. *Restaurants, Luncheonettes, Bakeries*

a) The owners should be *Shomrei Shabbos,* as well as trustworthy. *Shabbos* observance is a halachic measure of *Kashrus* reliability.

b) A reliable *Mashgiach (Kashrus* supervisor) should be on the premises if the owners/operators are not religious.

INTRODUCTION—KILAYIM

"You shall keep my statutes . . . you shall not sow your field with two kinds of seeds (Vayikra 19:9)"

"When you shall come into the land, and shall have planted all manner of trees for food, then you shall count the fruit thereof as forbidden; three years shall it be forbidden unto you; it shall not be eaten. And in the fourth year all the fruits thereof shall be holy; for giving praise unto Hashem (Vayikra 19:23, 24)."

1. It is forbidden to cross-breed all manner of plants *(Kilayim).* In the case of grains crossed with grapes, not only may the final product not be eaten, but no pleasure whatsoever may be derived from it.

2. The fruit which a tree bears during the first three years may not be enjoyed in any way. This is true of fruit grown either in or outside of *Eretz Yisroel.* In *Eretz Yisroel,* the fruit of the fourth year in Temple times used to be taken to Jerusalem and eaten in a ceremonial feast before the L-rd. Nowadays we redeem this fruit for a small coin. One should consult a *Rav* on the method of doing this.

INTRODUCTION—CHALLAH

"When you come into the land where I bring you, then it shall be that when you eat of the bread of the land you shall set apart a portion for a gift unto the L-rd. Of the first of your dough, you shall set apart a piece as a gift; as that which is set apart from the threshing floor (Terumah) *so shall you set it apart. Of the first of your dough shall you give a portion unto the L-rd for a gift , throughout your generations."* (Bamidbar)

but as soon as the man reached home, he complained of a stomach ailment, and from then on, lost his appetite so completely that he balked at the sight of food. Since he steadily lost weight and the doctors were baffled, his family seized upon the suggestion that some passerby offered them—that they should seek the advice of a certain *Tzaddik* who happened to be nearby at the time. His name: Reb Chaim of Sanz.

The *Tzaddik* heard their story and advised them to break all the *tre-*

1. After the produce of the fields is gathered in, it may not be put to use until G-d's ministers, the *Kohanim* and the *Leviim,* who possess no hereditary estates but devote themselves entirely to divine pursuits, are provided for. The *Terumah* and the *Ma'aser* must be separated and given to them. The laws of *Terumah* and *Ma'aser* are operative only in *Eretz Yisroel. Terumah* consists of a small portion of the harvest given to the *Kohein.* The next gift is the *Ma'aser,* a tithe, which must not be given by mere estimation, but must constitute a measured tenth of the produce. A second tithe is also separated, but its disposal is not always the same.

2. The separation of *Challah* is considered one of the duties and privileges of a Jewish wife.

A baker must remove as *Challah* one forty-eighth of his dough, while a housewife who bakes in smaller quantity must remove a greater portion, one twenty-fourth. Outside of *Eretz Yisroel* the custom is to remove from the dough a small portion the size of an olive and burn it. The minimum amount of dough which must be kneaded at one time in order that the separation of *Challah* be obligatory is a volume equal to that of forty-three and one-fifth eggs (from 3-5 pounds of flour). *Challah* must be taken only from dough prepared from the five kinds of grain: wheat, barley, oats, rye, and spelt. The obligation to separate *Challah* does not apply to flour, but to dough. Therefore, *Challah* separated before the water is added is of no account.

3. It is customary to wait until the end of the kneading before making the separation. In case one has failed to separate *Challah* from the dough, one must separate it from the bread after it has been baked. Upon the separation of the *Challah,* the following benediction should be recited: "Blessed art Thou, O L-rd our G-d, King of the Universe, Who hath hallowed us with His commandments and commanded us to separate the dough portion." *("Boruch Atoh Hashem . . . Asher Kidishonu . . . L'Hafrish Challah".)*

TEVILLAS KEYLIM

1. When one buys dishes or utensils of any kind from a gentile manufacturer, these must be immersed *(Toveled)* in a ritual bath *(Mik-*

fah (non-kosher) kitchen utensils in the house or sell them to gentiles. Then they should replace them with new ones and begin to keep a kosher kitchen. If they did that, he assured them, the head of the house would

soon be well.

As soon as these instructions were carried out, the waning patient indeed began recovering his appetite. As he regained his former strength, the reason for his ailment became clear to

veh). This applies to all glass, and metal utensils which is made for the purpose of containing food directly. This includes glassware, pots, pans, dishes, salad bowls, salad spoons, the toaster tray, or anything else on which food is placed directly. A tray that is used just for serving, where the food is not placed directly on it, does not have to be immersed. Earthenware does not have to be immersed except if it is coated with glass or glazed. Wood does not have to be immersed. A slaughter knife, which is used for *Shechita*, is questionable because it is used on something which has not yet become food for consumption. If these utensils are manufactured by a Jew, and remained under Jewish ownership, they do not have to be immersed.

2. If one buys aluminum disposable pans and has in mind to use them for a few times, they should be immersed. Bottles or jars which contain food when purchased, and then are used for storing food, do not have to be immersed, according to the Halachic decision of Rabbi Moshe Feinstein. This is because the jar or bottle was converted into a utensil by the Jewish person who bought the jar of food. If one obtains a utensil from a non-Jew and plans to return it, one does not have to immerse it. If one is offered a drink from a person whom one knows to be a gentile and who did not immerse his utensil or glass, one may drink from it nonetheless because it is not the Jew's glass and will not become so.

3. One must immerse the entire utensil in the water so that all parts, including the handle, are well immersed and can reach the water, he should hold it loosely to allow the water to touch all parts of it. A *Brocho* is required on the immersion of the utensil, except in those cases where it is questionable whether the utensil needs immersion, the *Brocho* that is made is *"Al Tevillas Keyli(m)"*. In more intricate cases, such as where the utensil is composed of two different materials, a *Rav* should be consulted.

---

them all: once he had tasted the sh'rayim which the *Tzaddik* had offered him, he had developed an instinctive aversion to any *trefah* food.

In 1923 the Chofetz Chaim felt that the community must be organized to provide kosher meals for Jewish soldiers. He called his new project *Kessel Kosher* (Kosher Kettle) and naturally, the first move he made was to travel to Vilna to secure the endorsement and support of the communal leaders. The

endorsement was not forthcoming. They felt that there were many overriding considerations making such a campaign inopportune at that time, and there were other priorities.

The Chofetz Chaim shrugged and replied, "What can I do? People consider me to be a G-d-fearing Jew. When I am called to the World-to-Come, they will ask me why I did nothing to provide kosher food for Jewish conscripts. What will I say?

FOOD FOR THOUGHT

1. There are some things which should not be eaten because the *Shulchan Oruch* tells us that they affect our health. Meat and fish should not be eaten together. In fact, one should rinse his mouth and wipe his hands between a course of fish and one of meat.

2. Foods left uncovered in the street (e.g. an open jar of food or bottle of soda) should not be eaten. Uncovered foods should not be left under the bed where a person sleeps. If they were, though, they may be eaten.

3. Any wine, meat or fish that was sent to a Jew via a gentile is ossur (prohibited) because it may have been exchanged for non-kosher food on the way. If it was sealed, packaged or marked in a fashion that shows that the item was not tampered with, and it also has a label, then it is permissible. (When traveling by plane, for example, one should make sure that the package of Kosher food given by the stewardess is completely sealed.)

4. Only fish that have scales and fins can be used. According to halacha, if fish fillets or strips are without the skins, a proper Rabbinic authority must attest to the fact that they come from a Kosher fish. In the absence of such supervision, the fish may not be used.

5. This poses a problem in the purchase of tuna fish and sardines, because the tuna fish usually comes in as skinned loins from the deep sea trawlers, and sardines are often packed as skinless and boneless.

6. In addition, many canned fishes contain added oils, broth and other flavoring sauces. The same supervision referred to above applies here as well.

7. Wine or grape juice that was handled by a gentile is called *Stom Yayin*. It is forbidden because gentiles used to use wine in the service of their idols. This prohibition remains in effect to this day. However, if the bottle of wine was double sealed, it is permissible. Also, wine that was cooked until it boiled (to such an extent that one cannot keep one's hand inside) *(Yayin Mevushol)* no longer comes under the heading of *Stom Yayin*. (At weddings and *Bar Mitzvah* celebrations where wine and

Perhaps I will tell them that I was not lazy or indifferent; I made the hard trip to Vilna even though I was weak and past eighty. But the leaders said I was wrong. Who knows better than those who are involved in what is right or wrong?"

The leaders knew they had been

champagne are served by non-Jews, it's best to use only those that have been cooked). After wine changes its form and becomes vinegar, and then the *Goy* touches it, it no longer comes under the prohibition of *Stom Yayin*. However, if the *Goy* touched the wine, before it turned to vinegar, it is still *ossur*.

bested. They called a public meeting in the central synagogue to be addressed by the Chofetz Chaim. At that time, *Kessel Kosher* was born.

כבוד

Kovod

KOVOD (Giving Honor)

KIBUD AV V'EM (Honoring Father and Mother)

"Honor your father and mother; so that your days may be prolonged upon the land which the L-rd, your G-d, has given you." (Shemos 20:12)

"You shall fear, every man, his mother and his father, and my Shabbos shall you keep; I am the L-rd your G-d." (Vayikroh 19:3)

One must be very careful about honoring one's father and mother. The reward for honoring parents is given both in this world and in the world to come.

KIBBUD AV V'EM

Besides the various laws regarding the correct observance of this precept, we are taught in our *Talmud* that the commandment requiring us to honor our parents continues even after their deaths. One of the many kindnesses of the Almighty is to forgive our ancestors 'their' sins, for the sake of 'our' deeds. How tragic is the custom to attend synagogue only for the sake of *Kaddish* (Mourner's Prayer), when the greatest respect we can actually pay our parents is to live a life which will serve as a credit and honor for them in the World-to-Come—i.e. a life based on the precepts of the Torah!

Our rabbis have taught us that the first five of the Ten Commandments are those dealing with the relationships of man to G-d, while the last five deal with relationships between man and his fellow man. This fifth commandment, "Honor your father and mother," is among those commandments between man and G-d, even though it appears to deal with a relationship between humans. The reason why it is in this group is to teach us that in order to truly fulfill the commandment to honor our parents, one must choose the path of Torah as his way of life.

"There are three partners in the creation of man: the Holy One Blessed be He, his father, and his mother. The sages taught that whenever a man honors his parents, it is as if he has brought down the Divine Presence to dwell with them and has honored G-d Himself. But whenever a man grieves his parents, G-d withholds His presence from among them so that He might not be grieved as well." (Kiddushin 30b)

"Mipneh Seivo Tokum" ("You

HILCHOS KIBUD AV V'EM

1. The Torah states that we must respect our parents. (The Torah uses the word "Yirah" which suggests a respect bordering on awe.)

One is not allowed to sit in the same place that is designated or reserved for one's parents.

2. One must stand up when a parent enters the room for the first time in the morning.

3. One should serve his parents cheerfully, by bringing them food and drink and other forms of comfort. If one can perform a task for his parents and thus make their lives more pleasant, he is thereby honoring them.

4. One is not allowed to call his parents by their first name, even when not in their presence. In fact, if your father is in the immediate area and there is somebody else whom you wish to call who has the same name as your father, it is best to call that person by his full name. This is done to show proper respect for one's parents. If his name is a common one, like Moshe or Dovid, many authorities hold that one is permitted to call someone else by that name.

should stand in front of old people and do honor in front of old men.") (Vayikra 19)

"It is a positive commandment to honor one's father and mother as it says, 'Honor your father and mother.'" (Shemos 20:12)

To appreciate the lengths that we should go to, in order to practice Kibbud Av V'em, we should remember the story of Damah, a gentile boy. Damah's father had a precious diamond which he kept under his pillow for its protection. One day, while his father was asleep, some businessmen came to Damah's house and asked to buy the diamond. Damah replied that he could not obtain the diamond, for to do so, he would have to wake his father and he did not want to do this. The men offered increasingly greater and greater sums of money, but Damah still refused to bother his father. Finally in desperation the men left and Damah lost his chance to make a for-

tune. Yet, for his devotion to his father, Damah received a just reward. Within his herd was born a Poroh Adumah, a totally red cow, needed by Jews for purity purposes, which he was able to sell at a very high price to these same people. He took only the cost of the actual loss of not selling the stone as his profit.

Damah also had a mother who had emotional problems, and who yelled and spit at him for no apparent reason. Though he was greatly embarrassed by her actions, he did not speak to her harshly. She was, after all his mother, despite all the hardships she caused him, he treated her royally. (Kiddushin 31a)

One day Rabbi Avuhu asked his son, Rabbi Avimi, for some water to drink. Rabbi Avimi brought the water, but his father had fallen asleep. He stood next to his father with the water in his hand the entire time, until he awoke. (Kiddushin 31b)

5. Even if one's parents become senile or mentally disturbed, and become a source of embarrassment, one is not allowed to treat them rudely or disrespectfully.

6. If someone curses his mother or father, even after their death, he has transgressed one of the severest *Mitzvos Lo Sa'aseh* (negative precepts of the Torah).

7. If one strikes his parents and draws blood, he has committed a crime punishable by strangulation. Even if he did not draw blood, he has still transgressed a *Lo Sa'aseh* (negative commandment).

8. The restriction against drawing blood goes so far that a child should not remove a splinter from, or open a blister of, his parent because this might cause bleeding. This, of course applies only in a case where there is someone else available to do it. If he is the only one who is able to help the parent at that time, he is obligated to do so.

9. Any assistance which one offers his parents should be done *B'sever Ponim Yofos* (in a pleasant, non-begrudging manner).

A man once came to Rabbi Chayim Solovetchik of Brisk with the following question: His father had become ill in a distant city and he felt obligated to take a trip to visit him. However, since it is questionable whether one is required to spend his own money to honor his father and the train trip would cost him a great deal of money, was he still obligated to go?

Rav Chaim's sharp reply was, "True, you aren't obligated to spend your own money on a train. Walk!!"

When Rabbi Leib of Kelm was a young man he once came home very late at night from the *Beis Hamedrash*. His parents were already sleeping, and he didn't have a key with him. He could not return to the *Beis Hamedrash* as it was closed for the night. In order not to awaken them, he remained in the street all night, despite the extreme cold.

Whenever his mother wanted to go to bed, Rabbi Tarfon would bend down and serve as a stool so that she could get on and off the bed. When he returned to the *Beis Medrash*, he seemed proud. They said to him, "You did not reach half the honor that you are supposed to give. Did she throw golden coins of yours into the sea without you then embarrassing her?-"(*Kiddushin* 31)

The mother of Rabbi Yishmael wanted to wash his feet and give him water when he came back from the *Beis Medrash*. Rabbi Yishmael refused to let her serve him. His mother went to one of the sages and complained that her son was not honoring her. When the sages asked Rabbi Yishmael about this, he said he did not want his mother to serve him. Thereupon, the sages commanded Rabbi Yishmael to let her do her will, which was his method of observing *Kibbud Em. (Yerushalmi Peah, Perek* 1)

*"These are the things that a person eats the fruit on in this world and the main reward comes in the next world: Honor your father and mother." (*Peah, Perek 1*)

"Cursed be he that holds in light*

125

WAYS OF HONORING ONE'S PARENTS

1. If a child cannot afford to support his needy parents he must still show them the proper *Derech Eretz* (respect) and do everything possible to ease their burden.

2. One is obligated to respect one's parents even after their deaths. For instance, one should repeat a thought or *D'var Torah* in his father's or mother's name. If it is within 12 months of their passing, some use the phrase *"Hareini Kaporas Mishkovo."* After 12 months, he says *"Zichrono Levrocho Lechayei Haolom Haboh."* (In Blessed Memory For A Life In The World To Come.)

3. One is not allowed to openly contradict one's parents. Even if he sees one of his parents transgressing a commandment of the Torah, he should not say, "You are committing an *aveiroh* (sin)." He should rather phrase it as if he were asking a question, "Father, doesn't the Torah say that this is not permissible?"

4. Although one must fear his father and be careful not to sit in his place, in certain instances, a father may relinquish the *kovod* (honor) that is due him. However, a father cannot condone any insult to himself.

esteem his father or his mother, and all the people shall say: Amen" (Devorim, 27:16)

"What does 'you should fear your father' mean? Do not sit in his place, do not speak for him and do not contradict his words." (Toras Kohanim)

"The Torah compares the Mitzvos *that we find the easiest to do to the* Mitzvos *that are much more difficult to observe. The easiest* Mitzvah *is sending the bird away. The most difficult* Mitzvah *to keep is honoring your father and mother and if you do these* Mitzvos *you will live·long."* (Yerushalmi Peah Perek 1)

KIBBUD RAV (Honoring One's Teacher)

The great *Tzaddik*, the Radiziner Rav, was living in Europe when the Nazis began their murderous rampage throughout Europe. As the butchers

approached, the Radiziner *Rebbe* began planning an escape for his fellow townfolk. Word of the plan leaked out, though, and the Rebbe was forced to flee. The Gestapo arrived in the town immediately and demanded his return. They laid down an ultimatum; either the Radiziner came forward, or the entire town population would be killed instead.

When the town's *Gabbai* heard of this, he hid the fact from his *Rebbe,* donned the Rebbe's white *Kittel* and his *Tallis,* and presented himself to the Germans. The Gestapo seized him and killed him instantly, believing him to be the *Rebbe.* He had sacrificed his own life to save his leader.

However, the Germans were soon informed of the trick. Their anger grew, and they delivered their final set of conditions: either the Rebbe emerged from hiding within two hours, or the people of the town would be taken out one by one and shot.

5. A son has to show respect to his father even if the son happens to be the Rav of the city.

6. The respect for one's father takes precedence over the respect accorded to one's grandfather. For example, if one has enough money to support only one person, he must support his father and mother before his grandparents.

7. One must also show respect to a stepmother, stepfather, father-in-law and mother-in-law.

8. A person must show respect for an older brother. We learn this from the posuk, *"Kabeid Es Ovicho V'Es Eemecho."* (Honor Your Father and Your Mother.) The *"vov"* from *"V'es"* which means, "and," is meant to include the honor due to one's older brother.

HONORING ONE'S REBBE (Teacher)

1. In addition to respecting one's parents, a person must respect and honor his *Rebbe.*

2. The respect due to one's *Rebbe* should be shown in every possible way. When he meets his *Rebbe,* he should greet the *Rebbe* in a special way, by saying "Hello *Rebbe,"* or *"Sholom Aleichim, Rebbe."*

3. One is not allowed to contradict his *Rebbe,* nor is he allowed to issue a *p'sak* (decision) in the presence of his *Rebbe.* This would be disrespectful.

The moment the *Rebbe* heard of this, he knew what he had to do. He left his refuge and declared, "I am the Radiziner. I am more than prepared to die in place of my fellow Jews, and to die in the service of *Hashem."* The remorseless Nazis dragged him in front of the town and murdered him on the spot. Before the final shots rang out, though, the *Rebbe* managed to cry out to his fellow townsfolk. "Do not surrender to these murderers. Resist. Remain loyal to *Hashem.* "Shema Yisroel Hashem Elokeinu Hashem Echod . . .!"

Rabbi Eleazar ben Shamua said: 'The fear of your teacher should be like the fear of G-d.' (Avos, 4:12)

Rabbi Hanina ben Para stated

that he who is angry with his teacher is considered angry with the L-rd. (Sanhedrin 110)

"It is a big sin to disgrace a sage or to hate him. Jerusalem was destroyed only because the people despised the sages. He who despises the sages has no share in the next world." (Shabbos 119b)

"The twelve thousand pairs of students of Rabbi Akiva died within a short time because they did not give honor to each other." (Yevomos 62b)

"He who passes upon a question of law in the presence of his teacher does not deserve to live." (Brochos 31b)

"He who stands up for old peo-

4. One must remember to give proper respect to his *Rebbe* because he is the one who has opened up before him the eternal world of wisdom and truth—*"Olam Ha-boh"* (the World-to-Come).

ple will merit the fear of G-d, as it says, 'You should stand up and fear G-d.'" (Sefer Charedim)

Rava said: 'He who loves scholars will have sons that are scholars; he who respects them, will have scholarly son-in-laws; he who reveres scholars will become a scholar himself.'" (Shabbos 23b)

צדקה
Tzedakah

INTRODUCTION—TZEDAKAH

"If there be among you a needy man, any one of your brethren within any of your gates in the land which the L-rd your G-d gives you; you shall not harden your heart, nor shut your hand unto him, and shall surely lend him sufficient for his need, you shall surely give him and you shall not give him with an ill grace; for because of this thing, the L-rd your G-d will bless you in all your work and in all to which you put your hand."
(Devorim 25: 7-8, 10)

It is a positive commandment to give charity to the poor people of the Jewish nation.

TZEDAKAH
CHARITY IN THE COLD

Rabbi Meisel was the *Av Beis Din* (head of the Jewish court) in the city of Lodz. He was beloved by the Jewish residents there, both for his leadership and for his concern for his fellow man. He was especially noted for his efforts to help the poor. For one thing, he personally donated large amounts of his own money to help them. Equally important, he gave up much of his free time to raise charity among the rich of the town.

One unusually cold winter night, Rabbi Meisel went from house to house in the better section of town, appealing for donations to help the poor people buy wood to heat their homes; people who might otherwise freeze to death. Rabbi Meisel was successful in collecting donations until he came to a mansion owned by a wealthy businessman, who was also exceptionally stingy. In the past, Rabbi Meisel had failed to get anything from this rich man, named Mr. Poznanski. This time, however, he was determined not to leave until he had succeeded in extracting a donation from him. Rabbi Meisel thought that if only Mr. Poznanski would realize what it is like to be poor. . . .

When Rabbi Meisel knocked on the door, a servant answered and asked him to enter. Instead he stood rooted to his spot on the doorstep and refused. "I am very tired from my travels, and I really can't go any further. Could you ask the honorable Mr. Poznanski to come out here to talk to me?"

Out of respect for the famous Rabbi, Mr. Poznanski, himself, came out and

HILCHOS TZEDAKAH

The Eight Levels of Giving Tzedakah

The *Rambam* (Maimonides) lists the following eight levels of *Tzedakah* (charity) in descending order of priority:

1. The highest level of giving *Tzedakah* is making someone self-sufficient so that he no longer has to go begging and is no longer a financial burden on the community. This can be done by giving him a present, lending him money to establish himself in business, finding him a job, or taking him into your own business.

2. The second level is giving *Tzedakah* without knowing to whom you are giving and without the recipient knowing from whom he is receiving. This is done by giving money through an intermediary, such as a *Gabbai Tzedakah* in *Shul*.

3. The third level is when the donor knows to whom he gives but the recipient does not know from whom he receives (e.g. sending money anonymously).

4. The fourth level is when the poor man knows who the donor is, but

asked, "My dear Rabbi, why are you standing out there in that cold? Why don't you come inside and let me give you some good hot tea." Seeing that the Rabbi would not budge, Mr. Poznanski came out to speak to him, asking what he could do for him.

Rabbi Meisel began to relate the desperate situation of the poor people in the town, who were without firewood to heat their homes. Then suddenly a blast of wind slammed the door shut and they were left standing outside with the door locked behind them. Despite Mr. Poznanski's protests that he had already given too much money for the poor, and if they weren't so lazy they would work harder and therefore have enough money, Rabbi Meisel continued to talk.

He noticed Mr. Poznanski slowly growing chilled, his teeth starting to chatter, and his face beginning to turn blue with cold. Finally, Mr. Poznanski suddenly lost his control and started banging on the door, screaming, "Help! Open up! If we don't get in soon, we'll turn into ice cubes." The butler came running to let them in. It took quite a while till Mr. Poznanski recovered from the cold. Finally Rabbi Meisel turned to him and said, "You were telling me about how the poor have no right to be cold," he said.

Mr. Poznanski looked at him in shame. He quickly pulled out his wallet and handed Rabbi Meisel a large sum of money. Rabbi Meisel smiled in satisfaction and told him. "Actually I waited outside so that you would join me and feel how it is to be poor and frozen. In this way you could be grateful to *Hashem* for what you have and more anxious to help the poor in the future."

"Not everyone who is rich today will be rich tomorrow and not everyone who is poor today will be poor tomorrow. Why? The world goes around in a circle." (Shemos, Rabbah, Parshas Shemos)

the donor doesn't know who the recipient is. An example of this is when a person sets up a fund for the purpose of distributing *Tzedakah* to the needy, but he himself doesn't know to whom the money will be given.

5. The fifth level is giving charity before the poor man has to embarrass himself by asking for it.

6. The sixth level is when an individual gives an appropriate amount when he is asked.

7. The seventh level is when one does not give the proper amount but nevertheless feels good about giving.

8. The lowest level is when one gives, but it pains him to do so. If he shows his unhappiness when giving to the poor man, he may not even get any reward for it at all.

GIVING CHARITY

1. A person should be happy about giving *Tzedakah*. It should be given in a way that causes the recipient the least amount of embarrassment and the greatest amount of happiness at the same time. Even if the person who is approached does not have money to give, he should still

"Hiding from giving charity is like serving idols." (Tosefta Peah, Perek 4)

"Happy is the person who stands firm in his faith during trials and tribulation. A poor person must accept punishment and not get angry; a rich person must give charity and not forget G-d even if he is rich. If they both withstand their tests, they will get this world and the next." (Shemos Rabbah).

STINGY SIMON

When the Gaon, Rabbi Yom Tov Lippman was rabbi of Krakow, Poland, there lived a very wealthy man in that city, known as "Stingy Simon." He was despised by all for he never gave any charity. On the other hand, his servant, Shloime, was known for his generosity and kindheartedness. After several years, Shloime retired from being the servant of "Stingy Simon." Then he had more spare time to help the poor and the needy.

One day, "Stingy Simon" passed away. No one in town mourned his passing and hardly anyone attended his funeral. As punishment for his niggardly behavior, he was buried in a corner section of the cemetery reserved for the wicked.

A short while later, Shloime ceased distributing charity. The poor who had depended on him were heartbroken. They appealed to Rabbi Lippman to speak to Shloime and find out what had happened. Why did he suddenly stop giving *Tzedakah?*

"Rabbi, now I can confess," said Shloime. "All these years that people praised *my* generosity and good heart, they did not know the true source of my funds."

"What do you mean?" asked the Rabbi. "I'm quite sure you didn't steal from anyone."

"Rabbi, I was under oath never to reveal the name of this great benefactor who wanted the privilege of fulfil-

comfort the poor person with words, for the Talmud says that giving comfort is even greater than giving *Tzedakah.*

2. One should give at least 1/10th *(Ma'aser)* of his income to *Tzedakah* in this way, but one should be careful to give within his means, i.e., one should not impoverish himself to the point that he must depend on others. However, even a poor person has a responsibility of giving *Tzedakah.*

3. There is great merit in giving *Tzedakah* in memory of a departed person, both for the donor and for the departed.

4. Some of the most important forms of *Tzedakah* include: giving to poor brides *(hachnossos kallah)*, giving to the sick, supporting children who learn Torah, and supporting *Bnei Torah.*

5. When giving *Tzedakah*, one should try to adhere to the following rules:

a) The first priority is to provide for one's own household, then for one's relatives (even if they are distant).

b) The poor within one's city take precedence over those of a distant city.

---

ling the great mitzvah of giving *Tzedakah* anonymously."

"But who was this generous benefactor? Let us thank him for his past assistance and perhaps he will continue to help the poor again in the future."

"I'm afraid that is not possible," said Shloime. "You see, 'Stingy Simon,' who lies buried in the corner section of the cemetery, has already passed on to his share in *Olam Haboh.* He distributed his entire fortune through my hands on condition that no one was to know its source. He simply did not seek honor or thanks. Now that he is gone, there is nothing left to give."

The Sage was astonished and impressed with the secret that Shloime had just revealed to him. The distinguished Rabbi Yom Tov Lippman then requested that upon his passing, he too, should be buried next to 'Stingy Simon,' the secret philanthropist of the city of Krakow.

"Each day G-d lauds the rich man who distributes charity in private." (Pesachim 112)

"Four things reverse an evil decree of man: charity, crying, changing of name and changing of action." (Rosh Hashonah 17)

RABBI MEISEL & THE CANDLESTICKS

A rabbi was once approached by a poor, elderly widow. "I ask your help, rabbi. I have been living in poverty ever since my husband died. Now my daughter is planning to get married. I do not want a fancy wedding, but do you know of anyone who can help me raise money for a dowry to support the young couple? I want them to start off their life together in happiness, not poverty."

The rabbi himself was hardly rich. He also had difficulty making ends meet. But when he heard the pleas of the woman, his own needs became secondary. He looked around the

c) In dealing with needy people outside of one's city, one should give top priority to the poor people of *Eretz Yisroel,* which has a law like the poor of one's city.

d) Feeding the hungry takes priority over providing clothing for the needy.

e) When both a man and a woman request assistance, one must first give to the woman because it is more difficult for her to go collecting. The same applies when giving *Tzedakah* to marry off poor orphans. One first gives to an orphaned bride and then to an orphaned groom.

f) One must also consider the status of the needy person. This applies both to giving *Tzedakah* and for *pidyon sh'vuyim* (redeeming captives). The order is: a) One's *Rebbe* or father b) *Talmid Chochom* c) a *Kohein* d) a *Levi* e) a *Yisroel.*

6. The greatest type of *Tzedakah,* and one of the greatest of all *Mitzvos,* is that of *pidyon sh'vuyim.* If one has bought bricks to build a Shul, one is allowed to sell those bricks in order to raise money for such a purpose. A person who is able to redeem someone else but doesn't do so, is guilty of committing many *aveiros* (sins), among them: *"Lo Sa'a-*

house, but could find little money. Then he had an inspiration. He went to a cabinet, and took out two sparkling silver objects. They were his wife's *Shabbos* candlesticks. He handed them to the widow. "Take these, please. When you sell them, make sure that you get a good price. And extend my very best to the young couple. I hope this helps them towards a blessed future."

The widow thanked the rabbi profusely; then she left. Soon it came time for the rabbi's wife to light the *Shabbos* candles. She came to the cabinet, opened it, and almost passed out. "The candlesticks!"

"I know, they are gone. I gave them to a widow to pay for her daughter's wedding."

"But they were solid silver!"

"All the better. That way, she can sell them for a fortune."

"But how will we serve G-d properly on Friday nights?"

"I think that G-d will understand," said the rabbi. "We merely used the candlesticks to perform another mitzvah. Besides, we don't need such luxuries to serve Him. We'll just get two potatoes, and stick the candles in them. Their glow will still be the same and maybe even brighter. *Hashem* will deem the *Mitzvah* of helping a widow marry off her child of greater worth than the possession of beautiful candlesticks, which we will be able to replace in a little while."

"There is no better medicine to live and win over the angel of death than the attribute of charity alone." (Tannah Dvai Eliyahu)

THE MERCIFUL ACT

The day before *Yom Kippur,* one of the wealthy men of the city of Brisk lost his fortune and was thrown into prison by his creditors. They announced they wouldn't release him

mod Al Dam Rei'acho" (You should not stand by while your friend's blood is spilled), and Sh'fichas Domim (spilling of blood).

7. When it comes to redeeming different people, redeeming women takes precedence over redeeming men.

8. The only time we question whether or not to redeem a person, is when the ransom is an exorbitant sum and we fear that by paying it once, we will set a precedent for other Jews to be held for very high ransom.

9. If all that the poor person requests is food to eat, one should give it immediately without asking questions. However, if the person requests a larger amount of money or additional assistance, one has the right to inquire about him.

10. A person should do all in his power to avoid having to ask for Tzedakah, even if this means taking a job that he may feel is below his dignity.

---

until they were repaid 5,000 rubles.

When Reb Chaim, the Rav of Brisk, heard this, he became deeply concerned and desperately tried to find a way to free the man.

On Yom Kippur eve, the Jews of Brisk gathered in Shul to recite Kol Nidrei. Suddenly, Reb Chaim arose and ascended the pulpit. "We cannot begin" he announced. A sudden hush spread like a wave over the congregants.

Reb Chaim faced the congregation. In a loud clear voice, he said, "One of our men is missing tonight. He is being held captive in prison because he couldn't pay 5,000 rubles. How can we expect the Almighty to have mercy on us if we do not show mercy to our own brother? Who will help us raise 5,000 rubles to ransom this captive?"

The members of the congregation responded warmly to his words, promising to bring in large sums of money immediately after Yom Kippur. In this way, more than 5,000 rubles were pledged.

Then Reb Chaim called out to his congregation. "Now I am certain that

Hashem will respond to our needs, just as we have responded to our brother's needs. Let us begin Kol Nidrei."

"He who does charity and kindness in this world is rewarded with peace, and has a mighty defense attorney between the Jews and their G-d." (Baba Basra 10)

RABBI BAMBERGER & THE SHOES

A poor man once came to Rabbi Bamberger, the Rav of Wuerzburg, while he was in the middle of learning in the Beis Hamedrash and told him that he needed shoes. Rabbi Bamberger promptly interrupted his learning and brought a pair of his own shoes for the needy person.

One of the students remarked that the shoes he gave away were just recently bought and the best he owned. "Why didn't you give him your old pair?"

"The poor man already has torn shoes. I should give him only the best," replied Rabbi Bamberger.

"There is nothing harder than poverty. He who is poor, it is as if he

11. A person who accepts *Tzedakah* when he really does not need it, will end up needing it. On the other hand, a person who really needs assistance and cannot survive without it, yet refuses to ask for it, is like one who commits suicide.

12. Although it is a great *Mitzvah* to give *Tzedakah b'Seser* (without disclosing the donor), if announcing the pledge publicly will encourage others to give more *Tzedakah*, then it is best to do so.

13. When one pledges to give *Tzedakah*, he must make sure to give it right away, for not fulfilling one's pledge is a very grave sin.

has all the pain in the world and as if all the curses are upon him. The Chazal *said, 'If you gathered all the pain on one side and poverty on the other side, poverty would tilt everything.'* " (Shemos Rabbah, Parshas Mishpotim)

THE OFFICER & THE MYSTERY MAN

The police officer was on his usual boring nightly route of checking the neighborhood one wet, rainy night. Suddenly he noticed a figure, clad all in black, lurking around one of the houses. He watched as the man, looking to all sides, ran on tiptoe up the front door of one of the houses. He noticed how the man took something from his pocket and quickly bent down. It seemed to the officer that a robbery was definitely in progress.

"Stop right where you are!" he shouted at the man, who quickly turned and tried to run away. But the officer was too quick and collared the man. The officer was surprised to see that it was an elderly man with a long beard. He tried questioning him but the man refused to answer anything and begged to be let go. Instead, the officer quickly rang the bell of the house where he had seen the man, despite all the old man's protests. Finally, the owner of the house came to the door to see what had happened.

"I just caught this man prowling outside your house. He seemed to be up to some mischief by the door. Do you recognize him?"

After looking closely at the old man, the owner seemed most amazed. He also noticed the old man trying to cover a small envelope on the floor with his foot. The owner turned to the officer and said, "Why, that's my own revered Rabbi, Rav Riff. I've known him for years, and he's the kindest man I've ever known. He's the last person on earth I'd ever suspect of stealing anything."

"Then why was he sneaking around here so late?" asked the officer. "And why is he trying to put his foot on that envelope there? Was he trying to slip in a bomb or something?"

The officer bent down to pick up the envelope. He could see that the Rabbi was turning very upset, but he opened the envelope anyway. Inside he found a large sum of money. That was all.

The officer was astounded. Then, the owner, suddenly realizing something, exclaimed, "Now I understand everything! You see, I used to be well-to-do until the recession hit my business. Since I was used to living well, it was especially difficult for me to adjust. I was too embarrassed to ask for help and didn't know what I would do next. Then, suddenly, one day, I found an

GABBAI TZEDAKAH (COLLECTOR OF CHARITY)

1. A *Gabbai Tzedakah* should be an honest, knowledgeable person and a *baal midos tovos* (one who possesses a good character). There should be two individuals responsible for the collection and three for distribution of *Tzedakah* so that there can never be any doubt regarding their actions.

2. A *Gabbai Tzedakah* should not collect so large a sum of money from children or from a wife that would cause a parent or husband to

envelope with money in it, outside my door. I didn't know what to do with it, so I kept it. Then a week or two later, I again found money. This continued for a long while, and I have always been very curious to know who was sending me the money. Well, now I know. The Rabbi, aware of my plight, was trying to save my pride by sending me the money anonymously."

The Rabbi's shy smile confirmed the story.

The officer quickly let go of the Rabbi's collar. "Well, sir, if that's the case, then please accept my apologies. I treated you like a criminal, and I was wrong. What I really should have done was to treat you like a king."

"Rabbi Yannai saw a man giving money to a poor person publicly. He said to him, 'Better not to give it, than to give it and to make the poor person ashamed.'" (Chagiga 5)

"Open your hand" means before the poor person comes; give it to him so that he does not get embarrassed." (Yalkut Yitzchok)

BENYOMIN THE VIRTUOUS

The Talmud relates that Benyomin the Virtuous was in charge of the public charity chest. One year, when a drought plagued the town, a woman came to him and begged for help. Although Benyomin felt sorry for the woman, there was no money left. The

woman, in desperation, cried, "If you do not help me, a woman and her seven children will surely die." Not wanting to bear the thought of this happening, Benyomin, who didn't have enough for himself, gave her money from his own pocket.

Some time later, Benyomin was seriously ill and the doctors had given up hope for his recovery. The ministering angels appeared before the Almighty and exclaimed, "Lord of the Universe, You have said that whoever saves one Jewish life is regarded as if he had saved the entire world. Should then Benyomin the Virtuous, who saved the lives of a woman and her seven children, die in the prime of his life?"

Immediately, the sentence of death was annulled, and instead, 22 years were added to Benyomin's life (*Bava Basra* 11a)

"What shall a man do to deserve children? Rabbi Eliezer advised: Let him distribute money among the poor. Rabbi Nechemia's disciples asked him: 'What have you done to prolong your life?' He answered, 'I have been generous with my money.'" (Megillah 28)

RABBI BORUCH BER LEIBOWITZ

A poor man once came to the home of Rabbi Boruch Ber Leibowitz to ask for a donation. Rabbi Leibowitz, who

object. If a woman has an independent source of income, then *Poskim* allow her to give a substantial sum besides her husband's donation *(Aruch Hashulchan, Hilchos Tzedakah* 248, Chapter 12).

3. A *Gabbai Tzedakah* should refrain from approaching a person who really cannot afford to donate, but would give only because he would be embarrassed to refuse.

was very poor himself, did not have any money to give. As the poor man left, Rav Boruch Ber accompanied him and they walked together quite a distance. When his disciples saw their teacher walking with the man, they joined him, and it was very noticeable that the poor man was overwhelmed by the honor being bestowed upon him.

Afterwards, Rabbi Leibowitz explained his behavior to his students. "A beggar humiliates himself because of the donation he expects to receive. If I am not able to give money, the least I can do is give him honor."

REB YESHAYA

A story is told of how the pious Rav Yeshaya practiced *hachnosos orchim* (inviting guests). Once a man and his wife were traveling through a village on *Erev Shabbos*, when they happened to notice a small house. Because they were very tired from their journey, they wanted to ask the owner for lodgings. However, they were afraid that the owner would ask too high a price for accommodating them. They were about to move on when the wheel on their carriage broke and they had no choice but to ask the owner for a place to stay for *Shabbos*.

When they knocked on the door, Rav Yeshaya answered and as soon as he heard of their plight, asked them inside. The man nervously asked Rav Yeshaya how much their accommodations would cost. Rav Yeshaya rep-

lied that it would cost five rubles, but that for this price they could eat as much food as they wanted.

The husband and wife decided that despite the fact that this was a high price, they had to accept it for lack of any alternative. At least this way they could eat as heartily as they desired.

As a result, they enjoyed the *Shabbos* meals very much, and they slept peacefully. When *Shabbos* was over, they felt that they had received more than their money's worth, and were most willing to pay the five rubles. However, Rav Yeshaya refused their money.

"But Rabbi," the man said, "we agreed on the price. We had a wonderful *Shabbos* here. Why then won't you accept our money?"

Rav Yeshaya replied, "Actually, I never had any intention of taking any money from you, as the *Mitzvah* of *hachnosos orchim* is one that I gladly perform for nothing. However, I sensed that if I told you at the outset that I wouldn't accept money, you would feel uncomfortable here and would not accept our hospitality. I wanted you to enjoy the *Shabbos*, and you did. That is payment enough."

REB HIRSH YERVITZ

Reb Hirsch Yervitz, the father-in-law of the Chasam Sofer, was a very wealthy man and he made sure to put his money to good use. He used to invite visitors to every *Shabbos* meal, in the spirit of *hachnosos orchim,* and

4. When a *Gabbai Tzedakah* allocates funds, he should take into consideration the needs and special circumstances of each individual. For example, a wealthy person who has become poor has more needs than one who has been poor all his life. The money that is distributed should be apportioned accordingly.

5. Although there is a set order that one is to follow when giving money of his own to the needy (see previous section), the *Gabbai Tzedakah* must be careful not to show favoritism, and he may not give his relatives precedence (because he serves as a representative of the community).

6. Anyone who collects *Tzedakah* has a double Mitzvah: Making sure the poor receive *Tzedakah*, and encouraging other people to give *Tzedakah*.

he made sure that the poor got especially good treatment.

One Friday night, he noticed that quite a lot of important guests had arrived. They were seated at a long table, with Reb Hirsch's place reserved at the front. But then Reb Hirsch noticed that two beggars had been assigned a place at the very end of the table. They looked quite forlorn, because it was obvious that they would be served last, and that they would receive the very least respect and recognition.

Reb Hirsch would not let such a situation go by without action. He immediately took his own setting, and the wine and the Challahs, and carried them to the other end of the table. Then he set them up there, and suddenly, the end of the table had become the front. The two beggars immediately perked up. Now they were the ones who had the seats of honor for the first time in their lives. And as for Reb Hirsch, it was the most joyous *Shabbos* meal he ever had.

SALTY SOUP

Rabbi Chaim of Sanz was once invited to dinner at the home of a wealthy man. The man went out of his

way to make sure that his holy guest would get the best possible service. He rang for the maid, and she brought in the soup portion first. The host insisted on Rabbi Chaim being served first. The Rabbi took a spoonful of the soup, and made a strange face. Then he noticed that the host was looking at him expectantly, and he smiled broadly. He proceeded to eat the soup very quickly, with obvious relish. Then, when the host was served, the Rabbi asked if he could have more and the host quickly gave him his own portion.

After the meal, one of the other guests came over to the Rabbi and asked him privately, "How could you eat two portions of the soup when it was so salty?"

Rabbi Chaim smiled. "The cook was obviously very nervous, and made the small mistake of putting too much salt into the soup. If my host had found out about it, the cook would certainly have been fired. How could I cause the cook to lose her job? So I quickly grabbed away the host's portion so that he wouldn't find out about it. This way the host was happy and the cook kept her job, so that was well worth the eating of a little salty soup."

138

בְּרִית מִילָה
Bris Milah

INTRODUCTION—BRIS MILAH

"And G-d said unto Abraham: 'And as for you, you shall keep My covenant, you and your seed after you, throughout their generations. This is My covenant which you shall keep, between Me and you and your seed after you: every male among you shall be circumcised, and you shall be circumcised in the flesh of your foreskin; and it shall be a token of a covenant between Me and you, and he that is eight days old shall be circumcised among you, every male throughout your generations, he that is born in the house . . . and My covenant shall be in your flesh for an everlasting covenant. And the uncircumcised male who is not circumcised in the flesh of his foreskin, that soul shall be cut off from his people; he has broken My covenant.' (Bereishis, 17:9-14)"

In the beginning of this chapter dealing with circumcision, G-d declared to Abraham, "I am G-d Almighty; walk before Me, and be wholehearted." (Bereishis 17:1) Our rabbis teach us that circumcision is the way in which the Jew expresses his "wholehearted" faith in Hashem.

THE SYMBOL

A person must never forget that his *Bris Milah* is a symbol and a reminder that he is spritually different from others. He must not be influenced by others who permit themselves to do whatever their hearts desire. Before doing anything, he must consider whether the action is one approved by the Torah.

Some people believe that the *Mitzvah* of *Bris Milah* was given for health purposes. Although this may be one of its reasons, we cannot view G-d's *Mitzvos* as mere health regulations. No one can know all the intentions of Hashem and all the reasons for His commandments. We, therefore, cannot explain a *Mitzvah* solely on the basis of human understanding. We are permitted to believe that Hashem's intention was to benefit our physical welfare, but we must not assume that this is the only reason for the *Mitzvah*. There is also a basic spiritual significance to it—it marks the baby's initiation into the pure and holy Chosen People.

Since *Bris Milah* is a *Mitzvah* and not merely a health practice, it must be performed by someone who is a competent *Mohel*. He must be well

HILCHOS BRIS MILAH

1. It is a positive commandment *(Mitzvos Assei)* for a father to circumcise his son *(Bris Milah)* when the child is eight days old. If the father is not competent to do so himself, he must see to it that someone else does it. If the father cannot or will not fulfill his obligation, then the mother, or any other party, must see to it that the *Bris* is performed.

2. It is important that the ceremony be performed at the proper time and in the proper manner. The *Bris* to take place on the eighth day of the infant's life, in the morning, after sunrise. If it is done at night, one has *not* fulfilled the obligation. In this case, a procedure called *Hatofas Dom Bris* must be done, wherein blood is drawn from that spot by a qualified *mohel.*

3. The foreskin must be completely removed. If the foreskin was not completely removed, this must be corrected.

4. The person performing the *Bris* should be righteous, skilled and familiar with all the laws pertaining to the *Bris.* The *Mohel* may not refuse to perform a *Bris* because of insufficient renumeration. If the *Bris* was performed by a non-Jew or a non-religious Jew, a *"Hatofas Dom Bris"* must be made.

5. The ceremony is normally performed with special instruments specifically designed for the circumcision. There are two stages to the *Milah:* (1) the cutting and (2) the separating of the lower skin *(periah).* Rav Moshe Feinstein, *Shlita,* says that these actions may be done, other authorities say it is better to do them separately. The *periah* is usually done with the finger nails. The lower skin is partly cut, and the remainder

acquainted with both the necessary medical techniques and the various religious laws required in the performance of this great *Mitzvah.*

Since G-d's people are different spiritually, He wanted them to be different physically also. By doing this *Mitzvah* of *Milah,* we are being separated from other people.

When Rabbi Shimon ben Gamliel's son was born, there existed harsh decrees against the Jews, one of which prohibited the *Bris Milah.* Those who performed a *Bris* on their children, were threatened with death. Nevertheless, Rabbi Shimon ben Gamliel

went ahead with the performance of this commandment.

The emperor soon heard rumors that Rabbi Shimon had disobeyed the law, and summoned him for a trial. He told them to bring along his son, so that he could check if the baby had undergone a *Bris.* On their way to the trial, Rabbi Shimon and his wife stopped at an inn and befriended a noble aristocratic family who were lodging there. The wife of the aristocrat had also just given birth to a child, and when she heard of Rabbi Shimon's plight, she offered to temporarily exchange her son for his.

is pushed back to join with the upper skin upon healing. After this, there is a drawing of blood *(metzitza)* which is important for the health of the child. A medication is then applied to the wound and it is covered with a bandage. The *orlah* (the circumcised piece of skin) is buried in sand.

6. The *Mohel* recites the blessing, *"Al HaMilah"* before the circumcision, and the father recites *"L'Hachneeso Bivreeso Shel Avrohom Ovinu"* immediately afterward. Both *Brochos* should be said while standing. If the father is not at the *Bris,* and there is a grandfather present, the latter should recite the *Brocho.* The guests present call out in Hebrew, "Just as the child has entered the covenant *(bris),* so too should he enter into a life of Torah, marriage and good deeds." *"Borai Pri Ha'Gofen"* is recited over the wine and a special *Brocho* is said in praise of the *Mitzvah* of *Milah.* The child is then named and a few drops of wine are placed in the mouth of the baby.

7. It is best to have ten adult Jewish males present at a *Bris.* Some people have a custom to recite the *"She'hechyanu"* blessing. The *Brochos* can be recited even though the baby's body is uncovered.

8. It is customary that a person should be a *sandik* (one who holds the child during the *Bris)* for no more than one child per family. Some say a *Rav* can be *Sandik* for two brothers. The reason why a *Rav* or *Talmid Chochom* is used many times as a *Sandik* is in order to inspire the child to emulate the *Sandik.*

There is a special seat at every *Bris* designated for Eliyahu the Prophet, and it is called the *Kisai Shel Eliyahu.*

9. After the *Bris* there is a *seudah* (festive meal). It is a *Mitzvah* to eat

Therefore, when ordered to present his baby, Rabbi Shimon displayed an obviously uncircumcized son. The charges against him were dismissed, and his child grew up to become the great Sage, Rabbi Yehuda Hanassi *(Tosfos, Avodah Zarah* 10b)

"Every Mitzvah *for which the Jews gave up their lives during the time of the decrees of the Greek and/or Roman governments, such as not serving idols and performing the* Milah, *is still carefully observed even today."* (Shabbos *130)*

During the Nazi persecution Rabbi Shapira, Rabbi of Prachnik, grandson of the holy Zadik of Bluzhov, was sawing a huge log with his weak hands in the midst of the forest of Janow, where the Jews from the ghetto had been herded for forest clearing. He sawed the wood with twisted hands, and emaciated arms, his body racked with hunger, to perform a task his Nazi persecutors called of "vital importance" to the great victory of the glorious Nazi regime over its inferior enemy.

The keen mind of the Rabbi of Prachnik was not functioning as faultlessly as would befit one of his genius. The saw, cutting deep into the great

and partake of this meal. The *seudah* should preferably take place in the daytime. If the *Bris* was performed on a fast day, the *seudah* is made at night.

10. On the first Friday night after a boy is born, there is a custom known as a *Sholom Zochor*. At this occasion, the friends and relatives of the parents visit them to join in celebrating the boy's birth.

11. A child should not have the *Bris* on the eighth day unless he is healthy. Otherwise the *Bris* is postponed until the *Mohel* determines that the baby is ready. If a baby is sick or has a fever, we even wait an extra seven days after the child gets well. One waits seven days after a baby has been removed from an incubator before performing the *Bris*. If the problem is with the child's weight, one does not wait seven days unless the *Mohel* feels that it is necessary. If the child is mildly jaundiced, requires an operation, or had brothers who had previously died due to their circumcision, a *Mohel* or *Rav* should be consulted.

12. If a child dies before he is eight days old, he is to have a *Bris* before being buried. An instrument other than the one that is normally used for a *Bris* is used to circumcise such a child. He is also given a name at that time.

13. It is customary not to name the child solely after someone who has died at an early age. Customarily, another name is added. Sephardic Jews name their children after living grandparents. A girl is named when the father is called to the Torah at the next reading of *Krias HaTorah*. Some wait until the *Shabbos* after the birth to announce the name. Some wait three days after the birth and some wait five days.

log, creaked agonizingly, and pain drove every thought from Rabbi Shapira's mind. It seemed to him as if flames of torment were whirling round in his head. Even his memories deserted him in the depths of this forest where the rifle-butts of the S.S. torturers had driven him. Who can picture the state of mind of a galley-slave, the hopeless apathy, in which the sufferer no longer remembers the past and no longer believes in the reality of the world?

Thousands of victims had been brought to the camp that day, among them many young mothers with infants in their arms. The older ones, the four and five years olds, played thoughtlessly in the shadow of death; but the mothers who realized that they had borne their children for the limepit, sat for hours on end, with misery etched in their eyes.

"What a devilish, foul crime," thought Rabbi Shapira's tortured mind. "To murder these innocent little children."

The saw ate its way into the log, when Rabbi Shapira heard steps approaching behind him. Involuntarily, he worked faster, because he was certain that an S.S. man was standing behind him. He glanced over his

14. *Tachanun* is not said on the day of a *Bris* by that congregation even if it is a *Ta'anis* (fast day). However, partial *Selichos* are said.

15. The *Milah* on a *mamzer* (illegitimate child) is performed in a different part of the Shul than that used for other circumcisions to indicate and announce the special status of the child.

16. On all fast days, the *Brocho* is recited over wine, and the wine is given to the baby or the parents when they don't have to fast. The Sephardim have a custom on *Yom Kippur* and *Tisha B'Av* of using *besamim* (spices) instead of wine.

17. If a person has twin boys, only one *Brocho* is said for both of them. However, if time has elapsed between the two *Brisos* and there has been talk of other things, then another *Brocho* must be recited. Other authorities say that an interruption should be made between the *Brisos* and two *Brochos* are recited. One should, therefore, consult a *Rav* in this case.

18. Even if the eighth day is *Shabbos,* the *Bris* is performed. Preparations that can be done before *Shabbos* must be done then. If they were not done, one can make the preparations only through a non-Jew or through a *sheenui* (a change from the usual manner) on *Shabbos*. For example, the knife should be brought to the house where the *Bris* is being performed, before *Shabbos*.

19. It is not permitted for a *Mohel* to travel in a vehicle on *Shabbos* in order to perform a *Bris*. A *Mohel* must perform a *Bris* even for people who do not keep the *Shabbos*.

20. An infant born through Caesarean section on *Shabbos* has his *Bris* on Sunday, the ninth day.

shoulder and, to his amazement, he saw a young Jewish mother with a little baby in her arms. How had this unfortunate, condemned woman gotten into the forest of Janow? How had she managed to come so far from the camp? Was she trying to escape? But the whole area was swarming with kapos and S.S. men! She could not even get a hundred yards from here!

But no, this unhappy young woman, was not trying to escape. On the contrary, she was coming towards him, seeking him.

"Have you a knife? Give it to me quickly, I beg you," she whispered, a wild defiance blazing in her eyes.

"A knife? For what purpose?" Rabbi Shapira asked in alarm.

"A knife!" she repeated over and over again, almost stubbornly, and he felt a strange resistance rising in his heart.

"I beg of you," he said. "Don't throw away your life, by killing yourself. Wait for your time to come. Perhaps before two hours are past, you shall share in the most exalted Jewish fate and die the death of a martyr. You shall die because your fathers, your forefathers, cherished an unshakable belief in the triumph of a pure and ethical life.

If a child is born *bein hashmoshos* (at dusk) and there is a question as to which day he was actually born on, the latter day is considered the birth date. If a child is born *bein hashmoshos* on *Erev Shabbos,* however, the *Bris* is performed on Sunday because of the *sofek* (doubt). The same would apply to *Yom Tov,* but, in all cases, a *Rav* should be consulted.

Centuries, thousands of years ago, they could have chosen the cruel, foolish way of life followed by other peoples, but they obeyed the will of the Creator Who conceived the thought of placing souls upon this earth, who represent the heavenly attributes of goodness and justice, and spread light throughout the world. For this special task, he found a race which replied, *"Na'aseh Venishma,"* we will accept the yoke, and we will shoulder it unconditionally. Then, Satan, angered by such boldness, resolved to fight this people, Israel. When at the time of the Cossack revolt in 1648, the blood of a hundred thousand Jews drenched the soil, the saintly Reb Samson Ostropoler spoke to the Satan:

'Listen, Satan, why do you not fight another people? Why do you always persecute unfortunate Israel?'

Satan's face broke into a truly devilish grin as he replied:

'I am willing to do so. Just give up to me the *Shabbos* and the commandment of the circumcision, and you will be free from me!'

" 'No, and a thousand times no,' proclaimed Reb Samson. 'Let millions and millions die, but we shall never depart one iota from the Commandments of the Torah.' So you see of what noble stock you have descended," continued Rabbi Shapira. "And you want to deprive yourself now of the merit of martyrdom before its consummation?"

No sooner had he concluded his explanation of the sin of suicide to the desperate Jewish woman, than he heard with consternation the sound of heavy S.S. boots behind him.

"Du Schwein! Du Hunt", the S.S. man shouted, beside himself with rage, and struck the Rabbi with his heavy fist. "Don't you know it is forbidden to speak to prisoners? Were you two conspiring against us?" he roared and hit the Rabbi again and again.

"No sir, this unfortunate woman asked me for a knife, obviously with the intention of killing herself, and I did all in my power to dissuade her. I did not want her to lose her salvation by committing such a grave sin."

The Nazi stopped his blows and looked incredulously at the rabbi who had fallen to the ground.

"What strange, fanatical people you are."

Lowering his voice, he turned to the trembling woman who pressed her child protectively to her bosom.

"Is it true what this Jew is saying?"

"It is the absolute truth," replied the woman. The fire blazing in her eyes seemed to drive sorrow from her face. "It is true that I asked this man for a knife, but I did not intend to kill myself with it. I needed it for another purpose."

"What purpose?"

The woman straightened up, radiating self-assurance and an almost transcendent pride. "We Jews have a

פדיון הבן
Pidyon Ha'ben

INTRODUCTION—PIDYON HA'BEN

". . . The first-born of man shall you surely redeem, . . . And their redemption-money—from a month old, shall you redeem them—shall be according to your valuation, five shekels of silver, after the shekel of the sanctuary—the same is twenty gerahs." (Bamidbar, 18: 15-16)

Since initially every first-born son belongs to Hashem, *it is the duty of every father to "buy him back" so that his child will not be required to physically be given back to* Hashem.

REDEMPTION OF THE FIRST-BORN

It is a Mitzvas Assei (positive commandment) for the father to be *podeh* (redeem) his *B'Chor* (first-born son). This is accomplished by giving a *Kohein* the equivalent of five *Shekels* of silver, declaring that this money is being given in exchange for his son. It has been determined that five old style (all silver) silver dollars contain the correct amount of silver, 96 grams, and are most often used for *Pidyon Ha'Ben*. Movable proper-

law," she said in a low but unhesitating voice, "that all male children are to be admitted into Abraham's Covenant. My little boy has not yet been circumcised. That was why I asked for a knife."

The pagan brute, who was perhaps a village school-master in civilian life, and who had taught German children the superiority of materialism, could hardly conceive that a downtrodden, wretched woman, condemned to death, should possess such fortitude. However, he did not want to seem sentimental.

"Idiotic fanaticism," he murmured.

"My child is a Jewish child. He was born a Jew, and I want to return him to

his Creator circumcised, in accordance with His command."

"I don't believe it," said the S.S. man. Then obeying a sudden impulse, he drew the bayonet and handed it to the woman with a cynical smile.

"Here, perhaps this will do for your purpose."

And the young Jewish woman stood in the middle of the forest of Janow, on the soil of a strange, accursed land, as if she had stepped out of the pages of the *Midrash*. They made the necessary preparations, then she fervently recited the benediction, and using the bayonet as a knife, the Rabbi circumcised the child.

"Amen," the rabbi responded to the

ties of equivalent value may be used instead, especially when silver coins are unavailable. Checks, dollar bills or base metal coins representing the correct value may not be used. This money is for the *Kohein* to keep. If he chooses to return it, he may, though it is preferable not to return it to the father. The *Kohein* may give the money to be kept in trust for the child.

1. The *Pidyon Ha'Ben* is performed after 30 days have elapsed since the birth, (the 31st day), and it should not be delayed or postponed. The ceremony may take place on *Chol Ha'moed,* but not on *Shabbos.* In the latter case, it is postponed until *Motzei Shabbos.* It is customary not to perform the *Pidyon Ha'Ben* at night. Since, one must take care that at least 29 days and 13 hours have elapsed since the birth of the child, which is sometimes not the case on the evening of the 31st day.

2. The father should perform the ceremony, for it is questionable whether it may be done through an agent. In a case where the father finds himself in circumstances which make it impossible for him to personally perform the *Pidyon Ha'Ben,* he should appoint an agent to do it for him. The agent should utilize the father's money for the *Pidyon.* (If the father is no longer alive, the child is to redeem himself when he is older. However, the custom is for someone else to do it for him on the 31st day.)

3. The father recites the *Brocho, "Baruch Ata Hashem Elokeinu Melech Ha'Olom Asher Kidishanu B'Mitzvosov V'Tzeevanu Al Pidyon Ha'Ben."*

blessing and his face too, was transfigured with joy.

"Amen," replied the Ministering Angels, and the ancestors, the great Jewish minds of all times. In that moment, the Jewish genius shone with a strength intensified a millionfold in the heavenly world.

"He who brings his son to Milah *is like a* Kohein Godol *who brings his* Mincha *and pours wine on the altar. This is why a person makes a party and is happy on the day that he merited to have* Milah *done to his son."* (Pirkey D'Rabbi Eliezer)

"R. Shimon ben Yochai said: 'Come and see how great the Jews are. There is no one a person loves *more than his son, and in order to do the will of his Creator, he sees his son undergo the pain of* Milah, *yet he accepts it with happiness.' R. Huna said, 'Furthermore, they spend money for a nice meal and make it also a day of happiness which was not commanded.'"* (Medrash Tehillim)

An Israeli soldier, wounded in the Suez Canal region and hospitalized in the Central Hospital in Beer Sheva, asked the surgeon taking care of him to circumcize him. The soldier, who immigrated to Israel with his parents five years previously from a European country, was not circumcised in his homeland and, upon immigrating, was

4. Someone whose father did not redeem him, should recite . . . *"Al Pidyon Ha'B'Chor,"* when he redeems himself.

5. The *Brocho, "Shehecheyanu"* is recited, the coins are given to the *Kohein,* counted, and then the *Kohein* recites a *Brocho* on wine. A seudo (ceremonial dinner) should be served for all guests present at the *Pidyon Ha'Ben.* It is considered a very joyous occasion.

6. If a *B'Chor* was sick and got well on the 31st day, a *Bris Milah* is performed first and then a *Pidyon.* If the child was still sick on the 31st day, a *Pidyon* is performed, even though the *Milah* was not yet performed and the name should then be given. However, others disagree with this opinion and make the *Pidyon* together with the *Bris.*

WHO DOES NEED A PIDYON HA'BEN

1. *Pidyon Ha'Ben* is not made for a child who did not live for 30 days. If a full term baby lived past 30 days and died afterwards, and no *Pidyon Ha'Ben* was made, the father must redeem his son nevertheless. The presence of the baby is not required for *Pidyon Ha'Ben,* but normally, the baby should be held during the ceremony if at all possible.

2. A child who is himself a *Kohein* or *Levi* does not need a *Pidyon.* A child whose mother is the daughter of a legitimate *Kohein* (one who did not marry a divorcee) or *Levi* does not need a *Pidyon.*

3. A child born to a daughter of a *Levi* who married a non-Jew does not need a *Pidyon Ha'Ben.* However, a child born to a daughter of a *Kohein* married to a non-Jew needs a *Pidyon Ha'Ben,* for the mother has lost her *Kehunah* status by marrying a gentile.

drafted and served in the Canal region. He had been wounded once before during the War of Attrition and had been hospitalized at this same place. At that time he had asked the same surgeon to circumcize him, but for a number of reasons it had not been done then.

When the *Yom Kippur* War began, he was called up with his reserve tank unit, which helped contain the advance in the Canal region. He was wounded and, when he regained consciousness, found himself at the hospital in Beer Sheva. He immediately called upon Dr. Abramovits, whom he remembered from his previous stay, and demanded that he be circumcised. His request was granted and the circumcision performed.

When he returned from the operating room, he was surprised by his fellow patients, who had prepared a small party for him in honor of the occasion. "Now I have a clear conscience and I shall leave the hospital as a complete Jew," he declared. The surgeon was overheard saying to himself: "I wish I had to perform only this kind of operation!"

"Avraham, our father, had Milah *on* Yom Kippur, *and every year G-d sees the blood of the* Bris *of Avraham our father and forgives*

4. If someone is unsure whether he is a *Kohein, Levi* or *Yisroel,* he is to have a *Pidyon* without a *Brocho.* This same *halacha* applies to one who does not know who his parents are.

5. A child born through Caesarean section does not have a *Pidyon Ha'Ben,* since it must be *Peter Rechem* (coming from the birth canal).

6. If there are twins, a male and female, and it is not definite which is the older, there is no *Pidyon;* however, if the twins are both males, then the father gives the *Kohein* the redemption money and declares that it should apply to whichever baby is the real *B'chor.*

7. A *mamzer* whose father is a *Kohein* or a *Levi* does *not* need a *Pidyon Ha'Ben.*

8. If a woman became a *geyores* (convert) after she became pregnant, a *Pidyon Ha'Ben* is performed if this is her first child.

9. A *Chollol* (the son of a *Kohein* married to a divorced woman) needs a *Pidyon* if his father dies within 30 days of his birth. This child is to redeem himself when he is older.

10. A child born after a miscarriage is not considered a *B'chor.* If the miscarriage was in the earliest stage of pregnancy or if the miscarried child was formless or otherwise mutilated, a competent *Rav* should be consulted.

all the sins of the Jews." (Pirkei D'Rabbi Eliezer *29).*

So eager was Reb Mordechai of Lechovitch to perform the *Mitzvah* of circumcision that he never once declined an invitation to act as *Mohel.* One short midwinter's day, on the *Shabbos* eve of *Chanuka,* he was honored by being able to perform two circumcisions in villages far apart from each other, one to the north of his town, and one to the south. When his *Chassidim* heard that he had accepted both invitations, they asked him whether he thought he could manage so much in such a short day.

He answered, "Regarding a certain passage in the Torah, the Talmud tells us that it comes to teach us of Avraham's enthusiasm which I understand to mean that the Torah teaches us of Avraham's zeal to implant it in us." And indeed Reb Mordechai rose at the crack of dawn, hastened to set out and circumcise the infants in both villages and sped home—weary, but in time to prepare for *Shabbos.*

We find that Moshe Rabbeinu who was such a close servant to Hashem, had almost suffered the punishment of death for not performing the *Bris Milah* of his son as early as he could. We see how important it is to perform the commandment of *Bris Milah* with fitting zeal.

Mezuzah

INTRODUCTION—MEZUZAH

It is a positive commandment to affix a Mezuzah on the doorposts of the house, as it says: (Devorim 6) "You should write on the doorposts of your house and on your gates." A Mezuzah contains two parshios (chapters)—"Shema" and "Vehoyo im Shemo'a." It is a Mitzvah that must be fulfilled during the day and night, by both men and women.

HILCHOS MEZUZAH

1. We must affix a *Mezuzah* to the doorposts of all our permanent dwellings. The parshios must be witten by a qualified *Sofer* (scribe) who must intend that it be used as a *Mezuzah*. The text must be written in special ink, in a single column of 22 lines, on a single piece of parchment.

2. The *Sofer* must first etch lines *(sirtut)* on the parchment to aid him in the writing. He must take care that every letter is properly written, for one incorrect letter ruins the entire *Mezuzah*.

3. The text must be written in its proper order from *"Shema"* until *"Ho'oretz."* There should be nothing added to the text (including inspection stamps of approval) once it is complete. On the back, the word,

THE MEZUZAH

Dovid Hamelech says in *Tehillim,* "Hashem Yishmor Tzaischoh U'voecho Mei'Atoh V'Ad Olam" ("Hashem will guard your going out and coming home, now and forever"). Hashem will guard him for the sake of the *Mezuzah* on his doorpost, not only while one is at home, but even while on is away from home.

"And you shall write them on the doorposts of your house and on your gates." The *Mitzvah* of *Mezuzah* clearly illustrates that not only are synagogues or other places of worship and study holy, but so too is one's home.

The sanctity of the Jewish home is symbolized by a *Mezuzah*, a small handwritten parchment scroll, affixed to the right doorpost of every room within the Jewish home. The *Mezuzah* also attests to *Hashem's* watchful care over His people.

Onkelos ben Kalonymous, a close relative of the Roman Emperor was not born Jewish. Nevertheless, he was attracted by the beauty of Judaism, and having sampled its teachings, decided to convert. The Emperor did

"Sha-dai" is written, and certain other letters are also added. The next-to-last line ends with *"Hashomayim,"* so that the last line contains only the words *"Al-Ho'oretz."*

4. The parchment is wound from left to right, so that the first word exposed upon unwinding it is *"Shema."* It is then placed in a protective encasement and affixed on the appropriate doorpost.

5. Immediately before affixing the *Mezuzah,* one should say the *Brocho* of *"Likvoa Mezuzah."* There is no *Brocho* of *"She'hecheyonu."* The *Mezuzah* should be affixed in a permanent position.

6. The *Mezuzah* should be placed on the doorpost which is on the righthand side upon entering from outside, regardless of whether members of the household are right-handed or left-handed. A doorway that leads to a backyard that has no other entrance (except through the

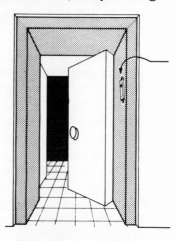

house) has the *Mezuzah* on the right side, going out from the house. If there is an entrance to the yard from the street, the *Mezuzah* is placed on the right side as one goes in from the yard to the home.

7. The *Mezuzah* must be placed in the upper third of the doorway, but not within the uppermost four inches. Some are careful to place the bottom of the case exactly higher than the average persons's shoulder, two-thirds the distance from the threshhold to the top of the door.

8. The *Mezuzah* should be placed at the outermost point of the doorway so as to include the entire room. It should be placed at an angle, with the top facing inside the room.

9. If there are two entrances to one room, both require *Mezuzahs.* At each entrance, the *Mezuzah* must be on the right side of the usual direction of entry. If it is not clear which room leads into which, the *Mezuzah* is placed on the right side of the direction into which the door opens.

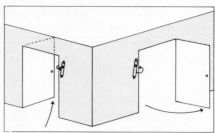

10. A *Mezuzah* is needed only if the doorway has two sideposts and a

top post. Therefore, if there is no right doorpost, or the posts are zigzag, there is no obligation for a *Mezuzah*. If there is a right doorpost, but no left doorpost, in a doorway whose left side is a continuous wall, one puts up a *Mezuzah* without making a *Brocho*. The term 'doorway' includes an opening in a wall flanked by the remaining sections of the wall. No door posts and jambs are necessary. (Figure one)

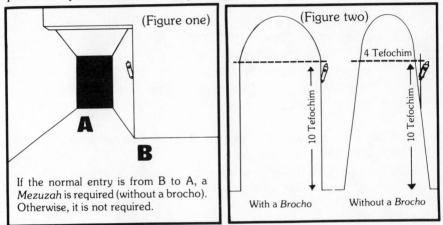

(Figure one)

If the normal entry is from B to A, a *Mezuzah* is required (without a brocho). Otherwise, it is not required.

(Figure two)

4 Tefochim

10 Tefochim

10 Tefochim

With a *Brocho*   Without a *Brocho*

11. The doorway must be at least ten *tefochim* high and four *tefochim* wide. (A *tefach* is between 3½ and 4 inches). If the top post is arched, there must be ten *tefochim* of height until the curve begins.

The dimensions of the room must be at least 4 *amos* by 4 *amos*. *(An amoh* is approximately 22 inches). If the area is 16 square *amos,* and one dimension is less than 4 (e.g., 2 *amos* by 8 *amos)* a *Mezuzah* should be placed on the door, but no *Brocho* is said. (Figure two)

12. The person putting up the *Mezuzah* should be over the age of *Bar-Mitzvah*.

13. A garage and a storage room require a *Mezuzah*.

not look upon this development kindly, considering it a threat to his own paganism. Consequently, he sent several groups of soldiers to Onkelos, demanding his return to Rome.

One group of soldiers was particularly determined to carry out the Emperor's charge. They came to Onkelos house, and insisted that he accompany them to Rome. Onkelos' words of praise for Judaism and his new life had no effect upon them at all. They almost dragged him out the door.

Suddenly though, Onkelos insisted that they stop. He went over to the doorpost of his house, raised his hand and placed it on a small box attached there. He then removed his hand and kissed it.

The soldiers gazed at him in astonishment. Onkelos smiled. "Do you see the difference between your human

14. The following do not need *Mezuzahs:* bathrooms, bath houses and other such rooms, temporary dwellings (such as a *Succah),* unroofed shacks and trapdoors that lie on the floor. Similarly a house in a neighborhood where one knows gentiles will remove and mutilate the *Mezuzah* has no *Chiyuv.* If at all possible, in this case the *Mezuzah* should be concealed inside the doorpost, but not buried to a depth of more than a *tefach.*

15. The following need a *Mezuzah* without a *Brocho:* a summer-only bungalow, a Shul or Yeshiva, a retail or wholesale store, and an office of employment. In these cases it is best to make a *Brocho* on a *Mezuzah* that definitely requires a *Brocho* and have in mind the others as well.

16. When more than one *Mezuzah* is affixed at a time, only one *Brocho* is recited. There must be no talk of other matters until the last *Mezuzah* is put on.

17. When a *Mezuzah* is exchanged or has fallen off, a new *Brocho* must be recited for its replacement.

18. A *Mezuzah* mistakenly attached to the left side should be re-attached to the right side, and a new *Brocho* should be recited at this time.

ruler and my G-d?" he said. "A human emperor stays inside his house, and his guards stand outside to watch over him. But my G-d stays at the door of the house and guards all the common people inside. This little box is a *Mezuzah,* and G-d's holy words are inside it, protecting those Jews who live in the house."

These words had a dramatic impact upon the soldiers. They had never before heard of such a leader, such a Supreme Power, and they too converted. The Emperor's command went unfulfilled. (*Avoda Zarah* 11a) And Onkelos the convert became one of the great names in Jewish history known to this very day as the author of the *Targum Onkelos (Megillah* 3a).

"*Rabbi Yehudah HaNossi told the king in regard to a* Mezuzah *he gave as a gift: 'The gift you sent me is so valuable that it will have to be guarded, while the gift I gave you*

will guard you, even when you are asleep!' " (Yerushalmi, Peah, Perek 1)

One would be well advised to spend money to get a *Mezuzah* that is more likely to be Kosher. Buying a small *Mezuzah* is highly risky, because it is very hard for a *Sofer* to write every part of every letter correctly on a small parchment. Care must also be taken to ascertain that the *Sofer* is a G-d fearing Jew who made the *Mezuzah* with the correct intentions *(l'shaim Mitzvah)* and fulfilled all the requirements.

When Reb Pinchas of Korets was still living in Ostrov, Reb Baruch of Mezibuzh was raised and educated in his house, and, after his marriage, Reb Baruch continued to visit his Rebbe frequently. He was once taking a nap in his Rebbe's room, when Reb Pinchas said to the people who were with him at the time: "If you stand around

19. Upon moving into a rented apartment in *Chutz l'Oretz* (a land outside Israel), with the intention of residing there for 30 days or more, it is best to affix *Mezuzahs* immediately without a *Brocho.* The *Brocho* is made on the 31st day, at which time one should remove the *Mezuzah* and replace it immediately. But most feel that simply holding it against the doorpost is enough. When one purchases his own home (in Israel or *Chutz l'Oretz)* he makes the *Brocho* on the first day.

20. Inasmuch as the *Mezuzah* contains two of the three portions of *"Krias Shema"* which is our pledge of allegiance to *Hashem,* it must be treated with respect. It should not be left on the floor or abused.

21. It is customary, when passing through a doorway, for one to touch the *Mezuzah* with one's right hand to show its importance.

22. When one moves from his house, he should not remove the *Mezuzahs* unless the new occupants are gentiles.

23. Women and children need *Mezuzahs* on their houses even when they live alone.

24. Mezuzahs must be examined by a *Sofer* at least twice in seven years to ensure that they have not deteriorated. A *Mezuzah* in a public place needs to be checked only twice in fifty years. A *Mezuzah* that is found to be *Possul* (spoiled) must be buried.

25. Although the *Mitzvah* of *Mezuzah* is an easy one to fulfill, the Torah promises great reward for it: *"Le'Maan Yirbu Yemeichem"* ("So that your days will be multiplied . . . heavenly days on earth"). People should acquire the finest *Mezuzahs* on the market. Whoever is diligent in this *Mitzvah* merits a befitting dwelling. *(Shabbos 23)*

my disciple's bed, I will show you something most unusual."

With that, he approached the doorpost of the bedroom, and with his hand, he covered the *Mezuzah* thereby blocking and separating the *Mezuzah* from Reb Baruch. Reb Baruch began at once to stir as if he was about to wake up, but the moment his Rebbe removed his hand from the *Mezuzah* he again fell soundly asleep. After Reb Pinchas had repeated this several times, he said, "You have now seen a man of true holiness. Even when Reb Baruch is asleep, his soul is not diverted from continuous cleaving to his Creator."

The *Mitzvah* of *Mezuzah* seems to be a small one in its actual fulfillment. It may cost only a few dollars, and we merely place it upon the entrance to our rooms. Yet, fulfilling this *Mitzvah* guides us in the most important principles and ideals of our faith.

Before reciting the blessing for affixing a *Mezuzah,* one recites the *"Y'hee Ratzon,"* stating, "Master of the Universe, look down from Your holy habitation and accept in mercy and favor the prayer of Your children who are gathered here to dedicate this dwelling and to offer their thanksgiving. Grant them that they may live in their home in brotherhood and friendship."

Glossary

Afikomen—last piece of matzoh eaten at the conclusion of the Passover seder meal

Agadah—homiletical portions of Talmud

Adar Rishon—first Adar

Adar Sheini—second Adar, occuring only in Hebrew leap years

Aliya—"going up" to recite blessing on Torah

Aleph Bais—Hebrew alphabet

Alos Hashachar—time when first rays of light appear in the east each morning

Am Ha'oretz—an unlearned man

Amidah—prayer of the 18 benedictions

Amos—cubits (each one approximately 22 inches)

Amud—lectern

Anshei Knesses Hagdolah—men of the great assembly

Aravos—willow branch

Aron Hakodesh—holy ark

Asseres Yemei Teshuva—10 days of penitence

Ashkenazim—Jews originating from North or Central Europe

Baal Agolah—wagon driver

Baal Habayis—head of the house

Baal Kriah—man who reads the Torah

Baal Midos Tovos—a person of good character

Baal Tokea—person who blows the Shofar

Bar Mitzvah—Jewish boy who turns 13

B'dee'eved—if already done, after the fact: see Mutar L'chatcheela

B'chor—first born son

Bedikas Chometz—search for chometz

Beis Din—rabbinical court of law

Beis Hamikdosh—Holy Temple

Beis Medrash—Torah study hall

Beitza—egg

Bein Hashmoshos—evening twilight

Ben—son

Bentch—bless, specifically saying the Birchos Hamozon

Ben Torah—a person who studies the Torah

Besomim—spices

Bimah—platform in synagogue used for reading of the Torah.

Birchas Hagomel—blessing of thanks to G-d

Birchos Hamazon—grace after meal

Birchos Hashachar—morning blessings

Birchos Hatorah—blessing of the Torah

Birchos Kohanim—blessing of the priests

Bishul Akum—food cooked by non-Jew

Bitul Chometz—nullifying chometz in one's possession before Pesach

Biy'mos Hamoshiach—in the days of the Messiah

Biyur Chometz—burning of chometz

Bnei Bayis—members of the household

Bnei Chorin—free men

Bosor B'cholov—meat and milk together

Briah Chadosho—new creation

Brocho—blessing

Brocho Acharono—blessing said after eating

Brocho L'Vatoloh—blessing said in vain

B'sesser—hidden

B'sever Ponim Yofos—with a pleasant face

Challah—braided bread made especially for the Sabbath

Chalom—dream

Chamar Hamedina—common beverage of the country

Charoses—mixture of wine, nuts and apples used on Pesach

Chatzee—half

Chassid—righteous one; adherent of a Chassidic sect

Chatzos—mid-point (noon or midnight)

Chazal—Talmudic Sages

Chazan—cantor

Chazoras Hashatz—repetition of the Shmoneh Esrei by the Shliach Tzeebur

Cheder—room (yeshiva)
Chessed—deeds of kindness
Chet—sin
Chidushim—original Torah commentaries
Chiyuv—necessity
Cholent—certain hot food cooked for Shabbos
Chol Hamoed—intermediate days of Pesach and Sukkos
Chollol—child born of a Kohein who married a divorcee
Cholov Akum—milk produced without Jewish supervision
Choson—groom
Chukim—unfathomable Mitzvos
Chumash—five books of the Pentateuch
Chutz La'oretz—lands outside of Eretz Yisroel
Chutzpah—audacity
Daven—pray
Derech Eretz—respect
Dinim—laws
D'Rabbonon—according to Rabbinic law
Duchan—the blessing of the Kohanim
D'var Torah—Torah thought
Echod—one
Egoz—nut
Ehrliche Yid—earnest Jew
Eiruv Tavshilin—symbolic dish making it permissible to cook on Yom Tov for Shabbos
Eliyahu Hanovi—Elijah the Prophet
Erev—day preceding
Esrog—citron
Ezras Noshim—women's section in Shul
Fleishig—meat product
Gabbai—1) synagogue attendant 2) collector of charity
Gam Zu Letova—it's all for the best
Gaon—Talmudic leader of post Talmudic era
Gartel—belt
Gebrukt—food containing matzo and water

Gedilim—strings prepared in the manner of Tzitzis
Gedolah—great
Gehenom—hell
Ger Tzedek—genuine convert
Geyores—convert to Judaism (female)
Gezeira—Rabbinic decree
Golus—exile
Hachnasass Kallah—mitzvah of supporting a bride
Hachnossas Orchim—receiving guests
Hachono—preparation
Hadassim—myrtle branches
Hafsokos—interruptions
Haftoro—passage from the Prophets read in the synagogue after the Pentateuchal reading
Hakodosh Boruch Hu—The Holy One Blessed Be He
Hakofos—dancing on Simchas Torah around the Bimah
Halacha—law
Hallel—prayer of praise to G-d
Hanetz Hachama—sunrise
Har Habayis—Temple Mount
Hashem—G-d
Hashem Yisboroach—G-d, Blessed be He
Hashgacha—supervision
Hashkomas Haboker—awakening in the morning
Hatofas Dom Bris—drawing of blood of circumcision
Havdalah—separation; Sabbath evening service to separate the Sabbath from the weekday
Hekdesh—sanctified for Temple use
Hashonnah Rabbah—7th day of Sukkos
Hiddur—enhancement, beautification
Hoshano—willow branches bound together
Ikur—basic principle
Im Yirtzah Hashem—if G-d is willing
Issur—prohibition
Kaddish—prayer recited by the chazon, or by mourners at various intervals during the service
Kaporo—forgiveness

Kashered—made kosher
Kedusha—holiness
Kehunah—priesthood
Kessel—kettle
Kezayis—amount the size of an olive
Kibbud Av'V'Em—respect for father and mother
Kiddush Levana—blessing made over the new moon each month
Kipah—skullcap
Kisei Shel Eliyahu—chair of Elijah
Kitniyos—beans
Kittel—long white coat worn at Seder and on Yom Kippur
K'laf—parchment
Klal Yisroel—nation of Israel
Kneidlach—matzoh balls
Koach Gavrah—by human power
Kochi V'otzem Yodi—done by own personal power (i.e. without Hashem's help)
Korach—sandwich of matzoh and morror
Kohein Godol—high priest
Korban Todoh—sacrificial offering of thanks
Kosel—wall, specifically wailing wall (Western Wall)
Kosher—ritually fit for use
Kovea Seuda—sit down formally to a meal
Kovod—respect
Krias Shema—reading of the Shema
Kugel—a pudding of baked noodles or potatoes made for Shabbos
Lag Baomer—33rd day of the Omer
L'Chayim—to life (used as a toast)
Lechem Mishneh—double portion of bread, used for Shabbos meals
Lechem Oni—poor man's bread (matzoh)
Laining—reading of the Torah
Lev—heart
Lishmah—purity of motivation (for its own sake)
Lo Saamod Al Dam Reyacho—exhortion not to stand by idly if another Jew is in danger

L'sheim Mitzvah—done for the purpose of performing a Mitzvah
L'Tzorech—for a necessity
Luach—calendar
Luchos—tablets of the Decalogue
Lulov—palm branch
L'vatoloh—in vain
Ma'ariv—evening prayer
Maaseh Bereishis—creation of the world and its inhabitants
Maaser—tithe
Machatzis Hashekel—half a shekel (coin)
Mafsik—interrupt by (talking)
Maftir—the last section of the Torah chapter read each week
Makom—place
Makom Kavuah—fixed place
Mamzer—illegitimate child
Matan Torah—giving of the Torah
Matonos Lo'evyonim—presents to the poor
Mayim Acharonim—water used to clean fingers before Birchos Hamazon
Mayim Rishonim—water for the washing of hands before the meal.
Mazal—luck
Med'orysoh—commanded in the Torah
Mechalel Shabbos—transgressor of the Shabbos
Mechila—forgiveness
Medrash—biblical exegesis
Midos—character traits
Melech—king
Mekabel—receive
Mekadesh—sanctify
Melava Malka—(post-Shabbos) Saturday evening meal
Melocho—work forbidden on Shabbos
Menorah—1) 8 branched candelabra used for the holiday of Chanukah 2) candelabra used in the Temple
Meoras Hamachpala—Cave of the Patriarchs
Meraglim—spies
Meshebeirach—a public blessing given for someone
Meshulach—fund raiser

Metzitza—extraction of blood by suction (circumcision)

Mevoreich—the one who recites the blessing

Mezuman—quorum of 3 adult males needed to say the Grace

Mezuzah—parchment inscribed with scriptural passages and attached to the doorpost

Midbar—desert

Mikveh—ritualarium

Milchig—milk product

Mincha—afternoon prayer

Minhag Hamakom—custom of the place

Minyan—quorum of 10 adult males needed for prayers

Misnagdim—opponents of the teachings of Chassidism

Mitzrayim—Egypt

Mitzvah Assei—positive commandment

Mitzvas Assei Shehazman Grommoh—ritual commandment performed only at specific times

Mitzvas Lo'Sa'aseh—Prohibitive Commandment

Mizbeiach—altar

Modeh Ani—morning prayer meaning "I thank you"

Mohel—circumcisor

Mohn—manna

Moled—monthly allignment of sun, moon and earth

Morror—bitter herbs

Moshol—parable

Motzee—1) to include others in the blessing 2) blessing over bread

Muktzeh—forbidden to be moved on Shabbos

Murkov—hybrid

"Mutar L'chatcheelah"—permissible before the fact

Naase V'Nishma—we will do and we will hear

Nedarim—promises, made in a ritually binding manner

Ner—candle

Neshama—soul

Neshama Yeseira—additional soul

Netilas Yodayim—ritual washing of the hands

Niftar—passed away

Nossi—civil and religious head of community

Novi—Prophet

Nusach Sefard—prayer arrangement according to the custom of Sefardim

Olam Habbah—the world to come

Oleh Al Shulchan Melochim—a dish worthy of being served to a King

Oleh Regel—pilgrimage to Jerusalem during the three holidays of Pesach, Shavuous and Succos

Olim—1) those called to the Torah 2) new immigrants to Eretz Yisroel

Omein—Amen

Oneg—pleasure

Ossur—forbidden

Orlah—1) foreskin removed during circumcision 2) fruits not eaten during the first three years of a tree's growth

Os—a sign

Ovel—mourner

Parsha—section of the Chumash read weekly

Pas Akum—bread baked by a gentile

Peleg Hamincha—final 1¼ hour period before nightfall

Perek—chapter

Periah—part of act of circumcision, peeling back of the lower foreskin

Pesach—Passover

Pesukei D'zimra—verses of praise taken from Psalms incorporated into daily Morning service

Pidyon Ha'Ben—redemption of the newborn

Pidyon Shevuyim—redemption of the captured

Pirsumei Neesah—publicizing the miracle

Pitum—protuberance opposite that of the stem

Podeh—redeem

Poroches—curtain for the Holy Ark

Possuk—biblical verse

Possul—invalid
P'sak—ruling
Purim—1) lots 2) holiday celebrating the victory of the Jews after Haman's evil plans to destroy them
Rabbosai Nevoreich—Gentlemen, let us say the Grace
Rav—rabbi
Rebbe—rabbi, teacher
Rekida—dance
Sakana—danger
Sandek—godfather at circumcision
Sanhedrin—supreme Rabbinical court of old
S'chach—covering of the Sukkah
Schnapps—whiskey
Seder—Passover meal
Sedra—weekly portion of the Torah
Sefardim—Jews originating in North Africa or Eastern countries
Sefer Torah—book of the Torah
Selichos—penitential prayers
Seudah—feast
Seudah Hamafsekes—last meal eaten before a fast (Yom Kippur and Tisha B'Av)
Sh'liach Tzeebur—messenger of the congregation, prayer leader
Shalach Monos—sending of gifts on Purim
Shalosh Seudos—third meal of the Sabbath
Shamas—sexton or beadle of a synagogue
Shamor—observe
Shavuous—festival commemorating the revelation at Sinai
Shechina—manifestation of the Divine Presence
Shechita—ritual slaughtering of animals
Shedra—spine
Sheebud Malchus—being enslaved by a foreign government
Shiur—required amount
Shekel—Hebrew coin
Shmoneh Esrei—silent prayer of 18 Benedictions
Shfichas Domim—spilling of blood

Shir Shel Yom—song of the day
Shiva—seven days of mourning
Shiva Minim—seven products which grow in Israel
Shkias Hachama—setting of the sun
Shlita—may he live long!
Shlug Kaporos—the ritual before Day of Atonement, performed with a live chicken
Shofar—ram's horn
Shoichet—ritual slaughterer
Sholeim—complete
Sholom Aleichim—peace be unto you
Sholom Zachor—welcome for a newborn boy
Shomrei Shabbos—Sabbath observers
Shtetel—small town
Shtiyos Hakos—drinking of the cup of wine
Shulchan Aruch—compilation of practical Torah law
Shul—synagogue
Shushan Purim—the day after Purim
Siddur—book of prayers
Simcha—happiness
Simchas Beis Hashoeivah—joyful drawing of the water performed in Beis Hamikdosh on Succos
Simchas Torah—holiday of rejoicing of the Torah
Siman Brocho—sign of blessing
Sinas Chinum—unwarranted hatred
Sippurei—stories
Sofer—scribe
So'oh—measure of volume: app. 3-4 gallons
Succas Ohr Shel Livyoson—Tabernacles made of Leviathan's skin to be erected after the coming of Messiah
Sukkos—Feast of Tabernacle
Stam Yayin—wine that came into contact with a gentile
Taanis—fast day
Tachanun—supplication
Tai'avon—appetite
Tallis Godol—prayer shawl
Tanach—scripture

Teenokos Shel Beis Rabban—small children who study Torah at school

Tefach—one sixth of a cubit: app. 3½ inches

Tefillah—prayers

Tefillas Haderech—traveler's prayer

Tefillin—phylacteries

Tefillin Shel Rosh—phylacteries placed on head

Tefillin Shel Yad—phylacteries placed on arm

Tehillim—Psalms

Tekios—blowings of the Shofar

Terumah—priestly portion

Teshuva—repentance

Teshuvos—responsa

Tish—table

Tisha B'Av—Fast of the ninth day of Av

Tnai—condition

Toch K'dei Dibbur—Halachic time measure—the time it takes to say "Sholom Aleichim Rabbi Umori"

Toluy—depends

Torah She'B'Al Peh—Oral law

Trief—not kosher

Tumah—ritual impurity

Tzaddikim—righteous men

Tzedakah—charity

Tzais Hakochavim—when the stars come out

Tzitzis—fringes worn at the corner of Tallis

Tzom—fast

Veeduy—confession

Yayin Pagum—wine from which people already drank

Yeshiva—Talmudic Academy

Yetzer Rah—the inclination to do evil

Yetzer Tov—the inclination to do good

Yirah—fear

Yiras Shomayim—fear of heaven

Yochid—single

Yahrtzeit—anniversary of death

Yom—day

Yomim Noroim—High Holy Days

Yom Kippur—Day of Atonement

Yom Tov—Holiday

Yotzai—to fulfill a Mitzvah or Brocho through another person's act

Yotzer Hameoros—Creater of the lights

Zachor—remember

Z'chus—merit

Zechuyos—merits

Zemiros—songs of Shabbos

Zeroah—roasted wing by the Passover table

Zimun—the joining of three males for Birchas Hamozon

Zman—time

Zman Kdei Achilas Pras—time span within which Kezayis must be eaten: app. 4-5 minutes

Zohar—the principle work of Kaballah